THE   BOOK   OF

CHICKEN
DISHES

T H E   B O O K   O F

CHICKEN
DISHES

KERENZA HARRIES & JO CRAIG

Photographed by
JON STEWART

HPBooks
a division of
PRICE STERN SLOAN
Los Angeles

ANOTHER BEST SELLING VOLUME FROM HPBOOKS

HPBooks
A division of Price Stern Sloan, Inc.
11150 Olympic Boulevard
Suite 650
Los Angeles, California 90064

9 8 7 6 5 4 3 2 1

By arrangement with Salamander Books Ltd.

© Salamander Books Ltd., 1993

Library of Congress Cataloging-in-Publication Data
Craig, Jo
   The book of chicken dishes/Jo Craig & Kerenza Harries.
      p.   cm.
   Includes index.
   ISBN 1-55788-075-1
   1. Cookery (Chicken)   I. Harries, Kerenza.   II. Title
TX750.5.C45C73   1993
641.6'65—dc20   93-8133
                                                   CIP

Home Economists: Kerenza Harries and Jo Craig
Printed in Belgium by Proost International Book Production

CONTENTS

INTRODUCTION

Chicken, as well as being a healthy alternative to red meat, is incredibly versatile – it can be cooked in dozens of interesting ways, and combines well with a whole host of other ingredients.

The Book of Chicken Dishes is an exciting collection of more than 100 recipes, some new and exotic, others classic, traditional and everyday, all equally delicious and easy. Each recipe is illustrated in full color with step-by-step directions. Many of the recipes call for chicken pieces and, although they are readily available, you may like to cut up a chicken yourself so you have the bones for making stock. The book starts with step-by-step directions showing how to do this.

Recipes reflect the distinctive flavors of Far Eastern, American and European cooking, starting with Soups & Starters and followed by Canapés & Finger Foods, Salads, Snacks, Classical Dishes, Tex-Mex & Far Eastern Dishes, Casseroles & Potpies and European Dishes. There are quick and simple lowfat recipes for everyday eating, and when you want to entertain, chicken is perfect combined with wine and cream or fruit, herbs or spices for a delicious and elegant dinner dish.

—— CUTTING UP A CHICKEN ——

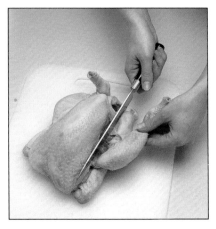

Pull the legs away from the chicken body and cut through the skin.

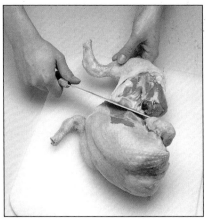

Bend the leg back to break the bone and cut through the socket. Repeat on the other side.

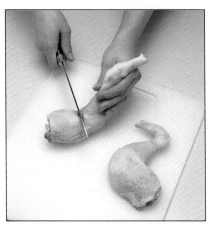

Hold the drumstick and cut through the socket to separate it from the thigh; cut the knuckle off the drumsticks.

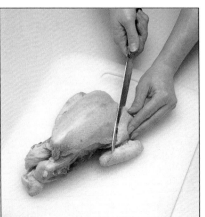

Pinch the lump of breast meat nearest to the wing, slice down and remove the wing completely.

Cut off the wing tip and fold the breast meat over the joint. Repeat with the other side.

Cut along the rib cage to separate the breast from the base of the carcass. You can use poultry shears to do this if you have them.

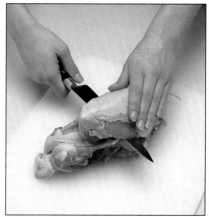

Cut the breast in half lengthwise to give 2 breast halves.

The chicken is now in 8 portions. Recipes in this book which specify skinned and boned chicken breast halves are using breast portions weighing about 4 ounces.

CONSOMMÉ

5 cups homemade chicken stock (see Note)
4 ounces chicken breast meat
2 large eggs
4 tablespoons finely chopped fresh parsley
1 teaspoon vegetable oil
salt and pepper

Into a large pan, put stock. Slowly bring to a boil. In a blender or food processor, finely chop chicken. Separate 1 egg and beat white lightly with a fork. Roughly crush shell. Mix together chicken, egg white, shell and 3 tablespoons of the parsley. Add to stock.

Bring stock to just below boiling, stirring. Reduce heat and simmer 25 minutes. Beat remaining egg with remaining yolk and parsley, and season with salt and pepper. In a small omelet pan, heat oil, pour in egg mixture and cook until set. Turn out and roll up like a jellyroll, then cut into thin strips. Strain soup through a sieve lined with cheesecloth. Pour into bowls and add strips of omelet.

Makes 4 servings.

Note: To make your own stock, into a large pan, put bones from a chicken, 1 quartered large onion, 2 halved carrots, 2 halved leeks, 2 sliced celery sticks, 1 bay leaf, some parsley stems, 1 bunch of thyme and 6 peppercorns with enough cold water to cover. Bring to a boil, then reduce heat and simmer 2 to 3 hours. Skim off any foam; strain into a large bowl. Cool as quickly as possible. Refrigerate until chilled, then remove any fat from surface. Use within 2 to 3 days or freeze up to 3 months.

——— HOT & SOUR SOUP ———

1 ounce dried Chinese mushrooms
3-3/4 cups chicken stock
1 ounce very thin egg noodles, roughly crushed
1 cup shredded cooked chicken
1 celery stalk, thinly sliced
2 small red chiles, seeded and sliced
2 teaspoons sugar
2 tablespoons cider vinegar
Pinch of white pepper
3 tablespoons dark soy sauce
1 tablespoon cornstarch
1 egg
1 tablespoon sesame oil
2 green onions, finely chopped
1 tablespoon finely chopped cilantro

In a small bowl, soak mushrooms in 1-1/4 cups of the stock 20 minutes. Drain, reserving any soaking liquor. Squeeze out any excess liquid and finely shred the mushrooms. Soak the noodles in the mushroom liquid 5 minutes. In a saucepan, bring all the stock and the reserved soaking liquid to a boil. Add the chicken, mushrooms, noodles, celery, chiles, sugar, vinegar, pepper and 2 tablespoons of the soy sauce and simmer 2 minutes.

In a saucepan, blend cornstarch with remaining soy sauce. Stir into soup; simmer, stirring, 2 minutes. Beat egg with the sesame oil. Whisking with a fork, pour into simmering soup in a fine stream. Stir in onions and cilantro. Serve at once.

Makes 4 servings.

—CREAM OF CHICKEN SOUP—

2 tablespoons butter or margarine
1 small leek, diced
1/3 cup all-purpose flour
3-3/4 cups chicken stock
2/3 cup dry white wine
1 cup finely chopped cooked chicken
Pinch of nutmeg
2/3 cup half and half
2 teaspoons snipped fresh chives
2/3 cup thick sour cream and croutons, to serve

In a saucepan, melt butter over low heat. Add leek; sauté until soft. Stir in flour. Cook over low heat 1 to 2 minutes.

Remove pan from heat. Slowly add stock, a little at a time, stirring well. Return to heat and bring to a boil, stirring until thickened.

Add wine. Cover and simmer 15 minutes. Add chicken and nutmeg and simmer 5 minutes longer. Pour in half and half and heat until hot without boiling. Stir in chives. Serve in warmed bowls with spoonfuls of sour cream and croutons.

Makes 4 servings.

—CORN & SHRIMP CHOWDER—

2 cups milk
2 cups chicken stock
2 cups whole-kernel corn
2 tablespoons butter or margarine
1 small onion, finely chopped
2 teaspoons all-purpose flour
1-1/3 cups finely cubed potato
1-1/3 cups finely diced cooked chicken
6 ounces shelled shrimp
2 tablespoons chopped fresh parsley
Salt and pepper
1/4 cup shredded Cheddar cheese

In a medium-size bowl, combine milk and stock.

In a blender or food processor, blend 1 cup corn in a little milk mixture until smooth. Add remaining milk mixture. In a pan, melt butter. Add onion; cook until softened. Stir in flour; cook 1 minute, stirring. Remove from heat. Stir in corn mixture, a little at a time, stirring well between each addition.

Return to heat. Bring to a boil, stirring constantly. Add potato. Simmer 15 minutes. Stir in remaining corn, chicken, shrimp and parsley. Season to taste. Sprinkle with cheese and serve with warm crusty bread.

Makes 4 servings.

COCK-A-LEEKIE SOUP

6 chicken thighs, skinned
4-1/2 cups chicken stock
3 leeks

In a large pan, put chicken thighs with chicken stock. Simmer 35 to 40 minutes.

Meanwhile, wash leeks; slice into rings. Remove cooked chicken from stock with a slotted spoon. Remove meat from bones. Cut meat into bite-size pieces. Set aside.

Increase heat and bring stock to a low boil. Add prepared leeks. Cook 3 to 4 minutes until leeks are just tender. Add chicken to pan and simmer 2 to 3 minutes. Serve hot with warm rolls.

Makes 4 servings.

CHICKEN SOUP WITH KREPLACH

2 cups all-purpose flour
Salt and pepper
3 eggs, beaten
2 tablespoons chopped fresh parsley
2 tablespoons chopped fresh oregano
1 tablespoon vegetable oil
1 small onion, finely chopped
6 ounces skinned and boned chicken, minced
Finely grated peel of lemon
2 tablespoons plain yogurt
2-1/2 cups canned chicken broth

Into a bowl, sift flour and a pinch of salt. Make a well in the center. Add eggs and 1 tablespoon each parsley and oregano.

Using a fork, gradually blend in flour to form a soft dough. If the dough is too sticky, add a little more flour. Knead dough on a lightly floured surface 3 to 4 minutes. Wrap in plastic wrap and refrigerate 30 minutes. In a small pan, heat oil. Add onion and cook until soft. Add minced chicken and cook 2 to 3 minutes longer. Add lemon, remaining herbs and yogurt. Season with a little salt and pepper; let cool. On a floured board, roll out the dough to about 1/8 inch thick. Cut into 2- to 2-1/2-inch squares.

Place 1 spoonful of filling on each square. Brush edges with a little water and fold dough in half over the filling to make a triangle. Pinch edges together to seal, then pull 2 corners together and pinch them to make them stick. Repeat with remaining dough and filling. Bring a pan of salted water to a boil. Add kreplach; cook 5 to 7 minutes or until the dough is cooked. Heat chicken broth, add kreplach, heat through and serve.

Makes 4 servings.

-CHICKEN & SHRIMP QUENELLES-

3/4 pound skinned and boned chicken breast halves
Salt and pepper
2 egg whites
2/3 cup whipping cream
1 cup chopped shelled cooked shrimp
2 ounces smoked salmon, finely chopped
1-1/4 cups chicken stock
1/4 cup plain yogurt
1 teaspoon cornstarch mixed with 1 tablespoon chicken
   stock
Grated peel and juice of 1/2 lemon
1 tablespoon chopped fresh dill
Lemon slices, lime slices and dill sprigs, to garnish

Into a blender or food processor, put chicken.
Process until minced.

With motor running, add salt and pepper,
egg whites and cream; process a few seconds
just until combined. Transfer to a medium-
size bowl. Very gently fold in shrimp and
smoked salmon. Cover and refrigerate 30
minutes. In a pan, bring chicken stock almost
to a simmer. Using 2 spoons, shape mixture
into neat quenelles. Slide into hot stock, in
batches. Simmer 1 to 2 minutes or until
quenelles are firm to touch. Remove from the
pan with a slotted spoon. Transfer to a dish,
cover with buttered foil and keep warm.
Cook remaining quenelles.

Increase heat and boil stock rapidly until
reduced by half. Stir in yogurt and cornstarch
mixture; cook over low heat, stirring, until
thickened. Add lemon peel and juice; season
with a little salt and pepper. Add chopped
dill. Pour the sauce over quenelles. Garnish
with lemon and lime slices and dill sprigs.
Serve hot.

Makes 4 servings.

RICOTTA-STUFFED MUSHROOMS

3 tablespoons olive oil
2 shallots, finely chopped
6 ounces skinned and boned chicken breast meat
1/2 cup ricotta cheese
4 tablespoons grated Parmesan cheese
8 pitted ripe olives, chopped
1/2 cup chopped pine nuts
2 tablespoons chopped fresh basil
1/4 teaspoon freshly grated nutmeg
Salt and pepper
8 large flat mushrooms

Preheat oven to 450F (230C). In a small pan, heat 1 tablespoon oil over medium-low heat. Add shallots; cook until soft and transparent.

In a food processor, process chicken until finely chopped; transfer to a bowl. Add ricotta cheese, 3 tablespoons of the Parmesan cheese, the olives, pine nuts, basil, shallots and nutmeg. Season with a little salt and pepper.

Put mushrooms, stem-ends up, in an oven-proof serving dish. Fill each one with chicken mixture. Sprinkle remaining oil and Parmesan cheese over filling. Bake 10 to 12 minutes or until lightly browned. Serve hot.

Makes 4 servings.

—— CHICKEN MOUSSELINES ——

12 ounces skinned and boned chicken breasts
2 tablespoons butter or margarine, softened
1 jumbo egg, beaten
2/3 cup whipping cream
1 tablespoon snipped fresh chives
1 teaspoon finely grated lemon peel
Salt and black pepper
Chopped bell pepper and parsley, to garnish
CHEESE FILLING:
1/3 cup pepper-coated soft cheese
2 teaspoons lemon juice
SAUCE:
2 red bell peppers, halved
1 ounce sun-dried tomatoes in oil, drained
3 tablespoons plain yogurt
1 teaspoon red-wine vinegar

Into a blender or food processor, place chicken and butter. Process until smooth. With motor running, pour in egg and 1/3 cup of the cream. Stir in chives, lemon peel, salt and black pepper. Spoon into 6 (1/2-cup) molds, tapping them well on countertop to level surface. For Cheese Filling: Cream together cheese, remaining 1/3 cup cream and the lemon juice. Put into a large pastry bag fitted with a large plain tip.

Plunge pastry tip deep into center of filled molds; pipe one-quarter of the filling into each. Use a wet finger to smooth chicken back over filling where the tip entered. Cover each with a small circle of parchment paper. Into a shallow pan half-filled with boiling water, place molds. Cover and simmer 15 minutes.

For Sauce, preheat broiler until very hot. Place pepper halves under preheated broiler; cook until skins are blackened. Let cool and peel.

In a blender or food processor, process peppers, tomatoes, yogurt and vinegar until smooth. Into a small pan, pour mixture. Heat until hot, stirring. Spoon some sauce on 6 small plates. Remove chicken mousselines from pan. Drain off any excess liquid which has collected in molds.

Peel off parchment paper. Turn out each mousseline on sauce on each plate. Serve at once, garnished with chopped pepper and parsley. Serve any extra sauce separately.

Makes 6 servings.

—CHICKEN & HAM MOUSSE—

1-1/3 cups finely ground cooked chicken
1 cup finely ground cooked ham
1 tablespoon fresh lemon juice
1 tablespoon chopped fresh parsley
1 tablespoon snipped fresh chives
2/3 cup mayonnaise
2 teaspoons unflavored gelatin powder
3 tablespoons chicken stock
2/3 cup whipping cream
Chives and lemon wedges, to garnish

In a bowl, mix chicken with ham, lemon juice, chopped herbs and mayonnaise.

In a small pan, sprinkle gelatin over chicken stock; leave 5 minutes to soften. Over low heat, melt very gently until gelatin dissolves, Remove from heat; cool. Fold into ham and chicken mixture.

In a medium-size bowl, with an electric mixer, lightly beat cream to form soft peaks. Carefully fold into chicken and ham mixture. Pour mixture into a 4-1/2-cup mold; cover and refrigerate 2 to 3 hours or until set. Unmold carefully on a plate and garnish with chives and lemons. Serve with hot crusty rolls.

Makes 4 servings.

— HOT CHICKEN LIVER MOUSSE —

8 ounces chicken livers
2 eggs
1/4 cup half and half
Salt and pepper
1 tablespoon vegetable oil
2 shallots, finely chopped
1/2 garlic clove, crushed
1 (7-oz.) can chopped tomatoes
6 tablespoons port wine
3 tablespoons Madeira wine
2 teaspoons tomato paste
1 teaspoon sugar
2/3 cup chicken stock
2 tablespoons butter or margarine
Chopped tomato and parsley leaf, to garnish

Preheat oven to 325F (160C). Remove membranes from chicken livers. Chop livers coarsely. Into a blender or food processor, put chicken livers with eggs, half and half, salt and pepper. Puree until smooth. Pour into a bowl, cover and refrigerate 30 minutes. Half-fill a roasting pan with boiling water. Lightly grease 4 (2/3-cup) ramekins. Pour mousse mixture into ramekins and place in roasting pan. Cover with greased foil. Bake 20 to 25 minutes or until mousse is firm.

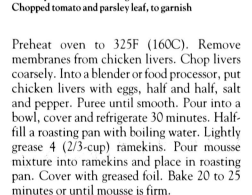

In a pan, heat oil. Add shallots and garlic; cook 1 to 2 minutes. Add tomatoes and cook 3 to 4 minutes longer. Add port wine and Madeira. Boil rapidly 1 minute. Add tomato paste, sugar and chicken stock. Season with salt and pepper, and simmer 10 to 12 minutes. In a blender or food processor, puree mixture. Return to pan and beat in the butter. Run a knife around edge of each ramekin. Turn out onto a plate. Spoon sauce around mousse, and garnish.

Makes 4 servings.

CHICKEN LIVER PÂTÉ

1 pound chicken livers
1 cup unsalted butter
1 garlic clove, crushed
2 tablespoons brandy
2 tablespoons port wine
Salt and pepper
2 tablespoons red currant jelly

Soak chicken livers in cold water 1 hour. Drain and remove membranes. In a skillet, heat 2 tablespoons of the butter. Add livers and fry 2 minutes, then add garlic and cook 2 to 3 minutes or until livers are cooked through, but still pink in center.

Cut remaining butter into cubes. Add to pan. Remove pan from heat. Leave butter to melt over livers. Meanwhile, into a small pan, put brandy and port wine. Boil rapidly about 1-1/2 minutes or until the liquid is reduced to a syrup; do not burn or the flavor of the pâté will be ruined.

Add wine mixture to livers. Season with salt and pepper and cool 15 minutes. Into a food processor or blender, put liver mixture. Blend until you have a smooth pate. Pour into 8 individual ramekins or 1 large serving dish. Melt red currant jelly and pour over pâté Cover and refrigerate at least 3 to 4 hours before serving.

Makes 8 servings.

—LAYERED COUNTRY TERRINE—

8 bacon slices
4 ounces chicken livers
4 ounces ground pork
4 ounces pork sausage
1 garlic clove
1 onion, finely chopped
3 tablespoons chopped fresh parsley
1/2 cup fresh white bread crumbs
1/4 cup brandy
1 egg, beaten
1/4 teaspoon freshly grated nutmeg
1 teaspoon finely grated lemon peel
Salt and pepper
2 skinned and boned chicken breast halves
1 bay leaf
Parsley, to garnish

Preheat oven to 350F (175C). On a chopping board, place bacon. Stretch with the back of a knife. Use 4 of the slices to line a 5-cup loaf pan, reserving 4 slices for top. With a sharp knife, roughly chop chicken livers. Mix together with pork, sausage, garlic, onion and parsley. In a small bowl, soak bread crumbs in brandy, then add to meat mixture. Beat in egg, nutmeg, lemon peel, salt and pepper.

Over bacon in pan, spread one-third of the meat mixture. Cut chicken into thin slices; layer half over meat mixture. Cover with half the remaining meat mixture, then cover with remaining chicken and remaining meat mixture. Lay reserved bacon on top and add bay leaf. Cover with foil. In a baking pan three-quarters full of boiling water, place terrine. Bake 1-1/2 hours. Remove from oven and cool. Cut into slices; garnish with parsley. Serve with crusty bread.

Makes 4 to 6 servings.

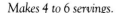

WRAPPED TERRINE

4 ounces large spinach leaves, stems removed
2 carrots, peeled
4 ounces green beans, trimmed
1 pound skinned and boned chicken meat
1 cup fresh white bread crumbs
1/3 cup whipping cream
4 teaspoons creamed horseradish sauce
2 teaspoons lemon juice
2 tablespoons dry sherry
1/4 teaspoon freshly grated nutmeg
Salt and pepper
2 eggs, separated
Garlic mayonnaise, to serve

Preheat oven to 350F (175C). In boiling water, blanch spinach leaves 30 seconds.

Plunge into cold water. Drain well; pat dry on paper towels. Cut carrots into even-sized sticks, about the same length as beans. Blanch carrots and beans 3 to 4 minutes in separate pans of boiling, salted water. Plunge into cold water to refresh; drain thoroughly. Into a blender or food processor, put chicken, bread crumbs, cream, horseradish, lemon juice, sherry, nutmeg, salt and pepper. Blend until smooth. Stir in the egg yolks and mix well.

In a medium-size bowl, beat egg whites until stiff but not dry. Fold into chicken mixture. Lightly oil a 5-cup loaf pan. Line with spinach leaves, slightly overlapping them each time and leaving enough to overhang the top rim of pan to cover top. Spread one-third of the chicken mixture over bottom of pan; level surface.

Cover with a neat layer of carrots. Top with half the remaining chicken mixture, then cover with a layer of beans.

Top with the final layer of chicken mixture. Fold overhanging spinach leaves neatly over the mixture. Cover with a piece of parchment paper and a layer of foil. In a deep baking pan, place loaf pan. Add enough boiling water to three-quarters fill baking pan.

Cook 50 minutes until firm. Leave to cool. Pour off any excess juices from pan. Turn out terrine onto a serving platter. Serve cold with a garlic mayonnaise.

Makes 6 servings.

ORIENTAL CHICKEN APPETIZERS

12 ounces skinned and boned chicken breast meat
2 tablespoons dry sherry
2 tablespoons soy sauce
2 tablespoons sesame oil
1 (1-inch) piece gingerroot, finely chopped
8 green onions, finely sliced
1 celery stalk, finely sliced
Vegetable oil for brushing

Cut chicken into 16 equal-size pieces. Put into a shallow dish. In a small bowl, mix together sherry, soy sauce and sesame oil. Pour over chicken and marinate 45 minutes.

Cut 16 squares of foil, each large enough to wrap around the piece of chicken. Brush each foil square with a little oil. On each foil square, put a piece of chicken. Top with a little of the gingerroot, onion and celery. Spoon any remaining marinade over chicken. Fold the foil over to make packages, making sure edges are well sealed.

Into a bamboo or metal steamer, place foil packages. Steam 10 minutes or until the chicken is cooked through.

Makes 4 servings.

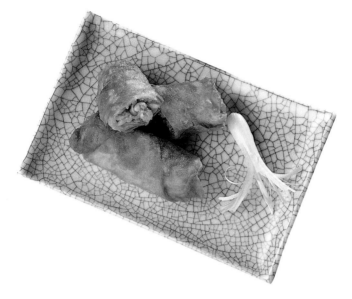

EGG ROLLS

2 tablespoons vegetable oil
1 garlic clove, finely chopped
1 (1-inch) piece gingerroot, finely chopped
4 ounces chicken breast meat, shredded
1/3 cup finely sliced snow peas
2-1/3 cups finely sliced shiitake mushrooms
8 green onions, finely chopped
1/2 cup chopped shelled, cooked shrimp
1 tablespoon soy sauce
1 teaspoon sesame oil
10 ounces filo pastry dough
1 egg white, for brushing
Vegetable oil, for deep frying
Green onion brushes, to garnish
Chile and hoisin sauce dips

In a wok or large skillet, heat the 2 tablespoons oil. Add garlic and gingerroot; stir-fry 15 seconds. Add chicken; stir-fry 2 to 3 minutes. Add snow peas, mushrooms, green onions and shrimp followed by the soy sauce and sesame oil. Mix well and transfer to a bowl to cool. Cut filo pastry dough into 16 (7-inch) squares. On a board, place a square with a corner toward you. Cover with another square of dough to make 2 layers.

Place 1 large tablespoon of mixture just below center of dough. Fold bottom corner over and then 2 side corners in to make an elongated open envelope. Brush dough with egg white and roll up, pressing gently. Repeat with remaining filo pastry dough and filling. Pour about 3 inches of oil into a deep pan; heat to 375F (190C) or until an 1-inch bread cube browns in 40 seconds. Add egg rolls in batches; fry about 4 minutes or until golden. Drain on paper towels. Serve with dips.

Makes 4 servings.

—— CHICKEN APRICOT BAGS ——

1/2 tablespoon vegetable oil, for frying, plus extra for
 brushing
1/2 onion, finely chopped
1/2 cup finely chopped dried apricots
1 cup finely diced cooked chicken
1/4 cup plain yogurt
2 tablespoons chopped fresh cilantro
Salt and pepper
3 sheets filo pastry dough
Watercress, to garnish

Preheat oven to 375F (190C). In a small pan,
heat the 1/2 tablespoon oil. Add onion; cook
3 to 4 minutes or until softened. Add chopped apricots and cook 2 minutes.

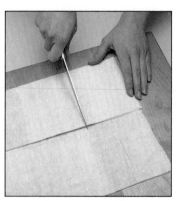

Into a bowl, put onion mixture. Add
chicken, yogurt, cilantro, salt and pepper;
mix well. Cut each sheet of filo pastry dough
in half, then cut each half into quarters to
make 16 (4-inch) squares.

Brush each dough square with a little oil.
Place a spoonful of chicken mixture in
center. Gather up corners of the square and
pinch together to form a loose bag. Place filo
bags on 2 baking sheets. Bake 10 to 12
minutes or until the dough is crisp and
golden. Serve warm. Garnish with
watercress.

Makes 16 appetizers.

—CHICKEN & BRIE TARTLETS—

3/4 cup all-purpose flour
2 tablespoons rice flour
4 teaspoons grated Parmesan cheese
1 teaspoon mustard powder
1/3 cup butter or margarine, chilled, diced
1 egg yolk
About 2 teaspoons cold water
FILLING:
1 cup diced cooked chicken
2/3 cup diced blue Cambazola cheese
16 asparagus spears
1 large egg
1/2 cup half and half
Salt and pepper

Preheat oven to 400F (205C). For pastry dough: Into a food processor, place flour, rice flour, Parmesan cheese, mustard and butter. Process 45 seconds or until mixture resembles coarse crumbs. Add egg yolk and 2 teaspoons water. Process until the dough binds together, adding a little more water, if necessary. Wrap in plastic wrap; refrigerate 15 to 20 minutes. Divide dough into four equal pieces. Roll out each piece on a floured surface and use to line 4-1/2-inch individual, loose-bottomed tart pans.

Arrange chicken and Cambazola cheese over bottom of each tartlet. Blanch asparagus in boiling salted water 2 minutes, then drain and refresh under cold running water. Pat dry on paper towels. Cut asparagus spears in half crosswise; arrange over chicken mixture. Beat together egg, half and half, salt and pepper. Divide equally among tartlets. Bake 25 minutes or until firm and set.

Makes 4 servings.

NUTTY CHICKEN STRIPS

12 ounces skinned and boned chicken breast meat
1/2 cup blanched almonds, finely ground
Fresh white bread crumbs
2 teaspoons finely chopped fresh parsley
1/4 cup all-purpose flour
Salt and pepper
1 large egg, beaten
Vegetable oil for deep-frying
2 tablespoons fruit chutney
1 tablespoon mayonnaise
1 teaspoon finely grated orange peel
1 tablespoon orange juice
Parsley and orange slices, to garnish

Cut chicken into thin strips. In a bowl, mix almonds, bread crumbs and parsley.

Into a large plastic bag, put flour, salt, pepper and chicken. Shake well. Dip chicken strips into beaten egg, then roll in bread crumb mixture to coat completely. Freeze 15 to 20 minutes. Pour about 3 inches of oil into a deep pan. Heat to 375F (190C) or until an 1-inch bread cube browns in 40 seconds. Add chicken strips, a few at a time; fry 3 to 4 minutes until golden-brown. Drain well on paper towels and keep warm while frying the remaining chicken.

In a small bowl, mix together chutney, mayonnaise, orange peel and juice. Spoon into a small serving dish. Garnish chicken with parsley and orange slices. Serve the sauce for dipping.

Makes 4 servings.

—DEVILED CHICKEN WINGS—

1 tablespoon vegetable oil
1 onion, chopped
1 garlic clove, crushed
1 (1-inch) piece gingerroot, peeled and finely chopped
1/2 teaspoon red (cayenne) pepper
1/2 teaspoon paprika
3 tablespoons red-wine vinegar
1/3 cup tomato ketchup
2 tablespoons brown sugar
2 tablespoons hot pepper sauce
2 teaspoons Dijon-style mustard
16 chicken wings

In a saucepan, heat oil. Add onion, garlic and gingerroot; cook until soft. Add spices

Cool 1 minute. Stir in vinegar, ketchup, brown sugar, hot sauce and mustard. Simmer 4 to 5 minutes, stirring occasionally. Preheat boiler.

Into a shallow flameproof dish or roasting pan, arrange chicken pieces; do not pack them too tightly. Pour sauce over chicken. Broil 12 to 15 minutes, turning and basting frequently with sauce, until crisp and brown.

Makes 4 servings.

—— ORIENTAL BACON ROLLS ——

1/2 pound chicken livers
2 teaspoons soy sauce
1 teaspoon finely chopped gingerroot
2 tablespoons honey
4 teaspoons dry sherry
8 bacon slices
8 canned water chestnuts, drained
Thyme sprigs, to garnish

Soak chicken livers in cold water 1 hour. Drain and remove membranes. Cut livers into 16 pieces.

In a bowl, mix together soy sauce, gingerroot, 2 teaspoons of the honey and the sherry. Add prepared chicken livers; marinate 25 minutes. Preheat broiler. Using the back of a knife, stretch each bacon slice, then cut in half.

With a knife, cut the water chestnuts in half. Place at end of a bacon slice. Top with a piece of liver and roll up bacon. Secure with a wooden pick. Continue until all the ingredients are used. Into a skillet or roasting pan, place bacon rolls. Pour remaining marinade over and drizzle with remaining honey. Broil until bacon is crisp and brown and the honey has caramelized. Serve hot; garnish with thyme.

Makes 16 appetizers.

SPINACH ROLL

1 tablespoon garlic-and-herb-flavored butter
1 (8-oz.) pkg. frozen spinach, thawed, drained
Salt and pepper
Freshly grated nutmeg
2 large eggs, separated
2 tablespoons grated Parmesan cheese
FILLING:
1/4 cup mayonnaise
1 tablespoon creamed horseradish sauce
1-1/3 cups finely shredded smoked chicken
1 teaspoon finely grated lemon peel
1 large red bell pepper, chopped
Watercress, to garnish

Preheat oven to 400F (205C). Grease a 13" × 9" baking pan; line with greased parchment paper. In a saucepan, melt butter. Add the spinach and cook 1 minute, then season with salt, pepper and nutmeg. In a blender or food processor, process spinach mixture until pureed. Add egg yolks; process to combine. In a small bowl, beat egg whites until stiff; gently fold into spinach mixture. Into prepared pan, spoon spinach mixture and level surface. Bake 7 to 10 minutes until springy to the touch.

Sprinkle Parmesan cheese over a large piece of parchment paper. Turn out roll onto parchment paper, remove lining paper, trim roll edges and roll up loosely. Let cool. In a small bowl, mix together mayonnaise, horseradish, chicken, lemon peel and chopped pepper. Unroll roll, spread with the chicken filling and re-roll. Cut into slices to serve. Garnish with watercress.

Makes 4 servings.

– CHICKEN & MANGO YAKITORI –

4 skinned and boned chicken breast halves
1 large ripe mango
1/3 cup chicken stock
1/3 cup sake or medium-sweet white wine
1/2 cup dark soy sauce
1-1/2 tablespoons brown sugar
2 tablespoons sweet sherry
1 garlic clove, crushed

Soak about 20 wooden skewers in water 30 minutes. With a sharp knife, cut chicken into long, thin strips about 1/4 inch wide. Peel mango; cut flesh seed, into 3/4-inch pieces. Thread a chicken strip onto a skewer, followed by a mango piece.

Wrap chicken over mango, then thread another piece of mango onto skewer; continue threading ingredients in this way so chicken weaves over and under mango. In a small pan, place all remaining ingredients. Cook, stirring, over low heat until the sugar has dissolved, then boil 1 minute. Set aside to cool. Preheat broiler.

Put a small amount of the sauce aside to use as a dip. Brush a little of the remaining sauce over kabobs. Place under hot broiler 30 seconds, then brush with a little more sauce and return to broiler 30 seconds longer. Repeat this process 2 to 3 minutes or until the kabobs are cooked through. Serve hot.

Makes 16 to 20 appetizers.

CHICKEN SATE

12 ounces skinned and boned chicken breasts, cut into
  long, thin strips
1 tablespoon grated gingerroot
1 teaspoon ground coriander
1 teaspoon turmeric
1-1/2 teaspoons chile powder
1 teaspoon brown sugar
2 tablespoons light soy sauce
2 tablespoons sesame oil
2 garlic cloves, crushed
Juice of 1 lime
1/2 cup chopped onion
2 ounces creamed coconut
2/3 cup boiling water
3 tablespoons crunchy peanut butter

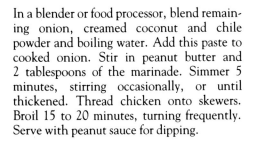

Arrange chicken in a shallow bowl. In a
blender or food processor, blend together
gingerroot, coriander, turmeric, 1/2 teaspoon
of the chile powder, sugar, soy sauce, 1 tablespoon of the sesame oil, garlic and lime juice.
Pour over chicken, cover and refrigerate 3 to
4 hours. To make sauce: In a skillet, heat
remaining 1 tablespoon sesame oil. Add half
of the onion; cook until softened. Preheat
broiler.

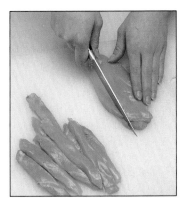

In a blender or food processor, blend remaining onion, creamed coconut and chile
powder and boiling water. Add this paste to
cooked onion. Stir in peanut butter and
2 tablespoons of the marinade. Simmer 5
minutes, stirring occasionally, or until
thickened. Thread chicken onto skewers.
Broil 15 to 20 minutes, turning frequently.
Serve with peanut sauce for dipping.

Makes 4 servings.

CLUB SANDWICH

12 bacon slices
12 white or whole-wheat bread slices
Butter or margarine, for spreading
3 chicken breast halves, cooked, thinly sliced
6 tablespoons mayonnaise
Freshly ground pepper
3 tomatoes, sliced
1/2 head Iceberg lettuce, shredded

Broil bacon until crisp, then drain on paper towels; keep warm. Toast bread. Spread one side with a little butter or margarine; keep warm. Mix together sliced chicken and mayonnaise.

To assemble sandwich, on a board, place 4 toast slices, buttered-sides up. Top with chicken mixture and spread evenly. Season with a little pepper and top each with another toast slice, buttered-side up.

To make second layer, cover each sandwich with 3 slices of bacon, sliced tomato and a little shredded lettuce. Season again with pepper and top with the 4 remaining toast slices, buttered-sides down. Insert 2 wooden picks into each sandwich, at opposite corners to help hold sandwich together. Carefully slice between picks to cut sandwiches.

Makes 4 servings.

——SESAME CHICKEN TOASTS——

2 large green onions
2 garlic cloves, crushed
1 (1-inch) piece gingerroot, finely chopped
1/3 pound skinned and boned chicken
2 tablespoons cornstarch
2 teaspoons light soy sauce
2 teaspoons oyster sauce
10 day-old white bread slices
1/3 cup sesame seeds
Vegetable oil, for frying
Green onion strips, to garnish

In a blender or food processor, process onions, garlic, gingerroot, chicken, cornstarch, soy and oyster sauces until smooth.

With a sharp knife, cut crusts off bread and spread each slice with a generous layer of chicken mixture. Sprinkle with a layer of sesame seeds. Place on a tray and refrigerate at least 20 minutes.

Pour 2 inches of oil into a deep pan. Heat to 375F (190C) or until an 1-inch bread cube browns in 40 seconds. Cut each topped bread slice into 3 pieces. Fry, a few at a time, until golden-brown. Drain on paper towels and serve hot. Garnish with green onion strips.

Makes 30 appetizers.

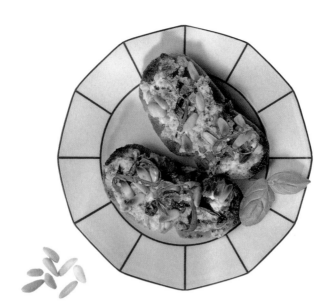

──ITALIAN LIVER TOASTS──

4 tablespoons oil from a jar of sun-dried tomatoes
1 garlic clove, crushed
1 small loaf Italian bread
4 ounces chicken livers, membranes removed and livers sliced
3 tablespoons prepared pesto sauce
1/2 cup ricotta cheese
4 teaspoons shredded basil leaves
4 teaspoons pine nuts
Basil leaves, to garnish

In a bowl, combine tomato oil and garlic. Set aside for flavors to blend 2 or 3 hours.

Preheat broiler. Slice bread into 1/2-inch-thick slices. Brush with oil. Toast under hot broiler until golden-brown. In a skillet, heat remaining oil and garlic. Add livers; fry until lightly browned. Stir in pesto sauce and remove from the heat.

In a bowl, break up ricotta cheese and fold in pesto mixture. Top each toast slice with liver mixture, sprinkle with a few basil shreds and some pine nuts and broil 1 minute or until bubbly. Serve at once, garnished with basil leaves.

Makes about 20 slices.

WALDORF SALAD

1/4 cup mayonnaise
2 tablespoons plain yogurt
1 tablespoon honey
Few drops of lemon juice
Salt and pepper
2 teaspoons snipped fresh chives
1 pound cooked chicken
6 ounces green seedless grapes
2 apples
2 celery stalks
1-1/3 cups walnut halves, toasted
Mixed salad greens
VINAIGRETTE:
1/4 cup olive oil
1 tablespoon lemon juice

In a medium-size bowl, mix together mayonnaise, yogurt and honey. Add lemon juice. Season with salt and pepper; stir in chopped chives. Remove skin from chicken and cut into thin strips. Cut grapes in half. Core and slice apples; chop celery. Add chicken, grapes, apples, celery and walnuts to mayonnaise mixture; stir gently to combine.

Make Vinaigrette: In a small bowl, beat together oil, lemon juice, salt and pepper. In a medium-size bowl, arrange salad greens. Add Vinaigrette; toss until greens are coated in dressing. Arrange salad greens on 4 plates and top with chicken mixture.

Makes 4 servings.

—MARINATED CHICKEN SALAD—

2/3 cup olive oil
4 tablespoons balsamic vinegar
2 tablespoons shredded fresh basil
2 tablespoons chopped fresh rosemary
2 garlic cloves, crushed
4 skinned and boned chicken breast halves
1 red bell pepper, quartered
1 yellow pepper, quartered
2 medium-size zucchini, cut into 1/2-inch-thick slices
2 large mushrooms
1/4 cup pine nuts, toasted
8 sun-dried tomatoes
1/2 teaspoon sugar
Salt and pepper

In a small bowl, mix together 4 tablespoons of the olive oil, 2 tablespoons of the vinegar, 1 tablespoon of the basil, 1 tablespoon of the rosemary and the garlic. Arrange chicken in a shallow, flameproof dish. Pour oil and herb mixture over chicken; marinate 30 minutes. Preheat broiler. Place dish of chicken under hot broiler; broil 10 to 14 minutes, turning halfway through, until chicken is brown and crispy. Set aside. Arrange peppers, zucchini and mushrooms in a broiler pan. Brush vegetables with 2 tablespoons oil; broil about 10 minutes, turning once, until cooked. Cool.

Using a sharp knife, peel skins from peppers. Cut mushrooms into quarters. Save any cooking juices from chicken. Slice chicken into 1-inch-thick slices and arrange with the broiled vegetables in a dish. Sprinkle with pine nuts and sun-dried tomatoes. In a small bowl, mix remaining herbs with oil, vinegar and any cooking juices from chicken. Add sugar, salt and pepper; stir to dissolve sugar. Pour over chicken. Marinate 1 hour, stirring occasionally.

Makes 4 servings.

— TROPICAL CHICKEN SALAD —

2 cooked smoked chicken breast halves, about 5 ounces
  each
2 ripe avocados
2 large ripe mangoes
1 head each of red and white Belgian endive
2 ounces arugula
3 tablespoons mayonnaise
1 teaspoon crushed pink peppercorns
1 tablespoon white-wine vinegar
3 tablespoons olive oil

With a sharp knife, cut chicken crosswise into thin slices. Remove skin and seed from avocados, then cut each half lengthwise into slices.

Cut mangoes in half by cutting on each side of seed. Peel and thinly slice. Separate endives into leaves and arrange with arugula on 4 plates. Place alternate slices of avocado and mango on top of the leaves and arrange one-quarter of the chicken slices on each serving.

Beat together mayonnaise, peppercorns, vinegar and oil. Drizzle over each salad. Serve with warm poppy seed rolls.

Makes 4 servings.

──── CHICKEN SATE SALAD ────

2 tablespoons dry sherry
1/4 cup crunchy peanut butter
1 (1-inch) piece gingerroot, finely chopped
2 tablespoons hoisin sauce
1 tablespoon fresh lemon juice
2 tablespoons dark soy sauce
2/3 cup chicken stock or water
1/4 cup sunflower seeds
2 teaspoons sesame oil
2 tablespoons vegetable oil
Salt and pepper
1 head Romaine lettuce, separated into leaves
1 cup bean sprouts
4 ounces green beans, cooked
4 skinned and boned chicken breasts halves

In a small bowl, mix together sherry, peanut butter, gingerroot, hoisin sauce, 2 teaspoons of the lemon juice and 1 tablespoon of the soy sauce. Slowly beat in stock or water; set aside. In a small pan over medium-high heat, put sunflower seeds. Cook, stirring constantly, about 1 minute or until seeds start to turn golden. Still stirring, add remaining 1 table-spoon soy sauce. The soy sauce will evaporate and coat the seeds. Turn seeds into a small bowl; cool. In a small bowl, mix together sesame oil, 1 tablespoon of the vegetable oil, remaining lemon juice, salt and pepper.

Into a bowl, place lettuce leaves and bean sprouts. Pour salad dressing over salad; toss to combine. Arrange lettuce mixture on 4 plates; set aside. Slice chicken into thin strips. In a skillet, heat remaining vegetable oil. Add chicken and stir-fry over high heat until chicken is golden-brown. Reduce heat and pour peanut butter mixture over chicken. Cook, stirring, until sauce is thick, adding more stock, if necessary. Spoon over lettuce; sprinkle with the sunflower seeds.

Makes 4 servings.

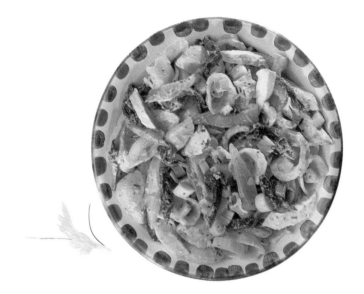

CHICKEN PASTA SALAD

1 garlic clove, crushed
2 teaspoons whole-grain mustard
1 teaspoon honey
3 tablespoons olive oil
1/2 cup snipped chives plus extra to serve
2/3 cup plain yogurt
Large pinch of saffron strands
3-3/4 cups chicken stock
2 skinned and boned chicken breast halves
1-1/4 cups pasta shapes
3 yellow bell peppers, halved
2 ounces sun-dried tomatoes
6 green onions
1 celery heart, with leaves
Salt and black pepper

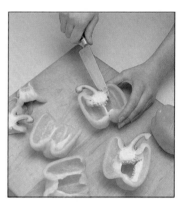

In a medium-size bowl, beat together garlic, mustard, honey, vinegar, oil, the 1/2 cup chives and yogurt; set dressing aside. In a pan, soak saffron in chicken stock. Bring to a boil, then reduce heat to simmer. Add chicken breasts and poach gently 15 minutes. Remove chicken with tongs; set aside to cool slightly. Add pasta to poaching liquid; cook 8 to 10 minutes or until pasta is tender, yet firm to the bite. Drain well. Add to dressing; toss to combine.

Preheat broiler. Place bell peppers, cut-sides down, on a baking pan. Broil until the skins blacken and blister. Cool, then peel off blackened skins. Cut peeled peppers into thick strips and stir into pasta. Cut chicken into strips, slice tomatoes, green onions and celery hearts. Stir into pasta. Season to taste with salt and plenty of black pepper. Sprinkle with remaining chives and serve warm or chilled.

Makes 4 servings.

– WARM CHICKEN LIVER SALAD –

6 ounces small spinach leaves
1 small radicchio, separated into leaves
2 oranges, cut into segments
1 red onion, sliced into rings
2 tablespoons butter or margarine
1 tablespoon hazelnut oil
1 pound chicken livers, membranes removed and livers
    halved
1 garlic clove, crushed
1 tablespoon sherry vinegar
1-1/2 teaspoons whole-grain mustard
3 tablespoons dry sherry
1 teaspoon honey
Salt and pepper
2 tablespoons coarsely chopped toasted hazelnuts, to
    garnish

Arrange spinach and radicchio leaves on 4 plates. Arrange orange segments and onion rings over greens.

In a heavy-bottomed skillet, heat butter and oil. Add chicken livers and cook, stirring, over high heat until well browned. Push livers to side of pan, then add garlic, vinegar, mustard, sherry, honey, salt and pepper. Bring to a boil; cook until reduced slightly. Stir in livers. Spoon livers over salad. Sprinkle with chopped toasted hazelnuts.

Makes 4 servings.

SPICY THAI SALAD

2 teaspoons sesame oil
2 red chiles, seeded and chopped
1 garlic clove, crushed
Juice of 1 lime
2 teaspoons brown sugar
1 tablespoon fish sauce
1 stem lemon grass, chopped
2 tablespoons shredded basil
2 cups shredded cooked chicken
2 ounces rice noodles
4 green onions, cut into matchstick strips
1 large carrot, cut into matchstick strips
1 yellow bell pepper, cut into matchstick strips
3 Napa cabbage leaves, shredded
2 tablespoons dry roasted peanuts, chopped

In a small pan, heat oil over high heat. Add chiles and garlic; cook, stirring, until softened. Remove from heat and stir in lime juice, sugar, fish sauce, lemon grass and basil. Pour mixture over shredded chicken and let stand 30 minutes.

Cook rice noodles according to package directions. Drain and rinse well in cold water. Drain well again. In a large bowl, mix together noodles, onions, carrot, bell pepper and cabbage. Spoon chicken and sauce over noodle mixture. Sprinkle with chopped peanuts.

Makes 4 servings.

—CURRIED CHICKEN SALAD—

1 tablespoon olive oil
1 small onion, diced
2 teaspoons mild curry paste
1 (7-oz.) can chopped tomatoes
1/4 cup dry white wine
2 tablespoons hot mango chutney, chopped if necessary
2 teaspoons apricot jam
2 teaspoons fresh lemon juice
2/3 cup mayonnaise
2/3 cup plain yogurt
1 pound cooked chicken
2 cups cooked, long-grain rice
1 red bell pepper, diced
2 tablespoons chopped fresh mint
3 tablespoons prepared Italian salad dressing

In a small saucepan, heat oil. Add onion; cook until softened but not browned. Stir in curry paste, tomatoes and wine. Bring to a boil. Reduce heat and simmer 15 minutes. Stir in chutney, jam and lemon juice; cook, stirring occasionally, 5 minutes or until thick and syrupy.

Remove from heat. Strain into a small bowl; set aside to cool. When completely cold, stir in mayonnaise and yogurt and mix well. Cut the chicken into large pieces and stir into sauce. In a medium-size bowl, combine rice, bell pepper, mint and dressing. Spoon rice mixture into a large serving dish; arrange chicken in center of rice.

Makes 4 servings.

—MEXICAN CHICKEN SALAD—

2/3 cup canned kidney beans, drained
2/3 cup canned chickpeas, drained
1 red bell pepper, cut into strips
1 head leaf lettuce, shredded
1 tablespoon prepared mustard
2 teaspoons sugar
2 tablespoons red-wine vinegar
2/3 cup olive oil
Salt and pepper
4 teaspoons paprika
2 teaspoons red (cayenne) pepper
1 teaspoon chili powder
4 skinned and boned chicken breast halves, cut into
   strips
2 tablespoons vegetable oil

In a large bowl, mix together kidney beans, chickpeas, bell pepper and shredded lettuce. Arrange on 4 plates. In a bowl, beat together mustard, sugar and vinegar. Slowly drizzle in olive oil, whisking all the time to make a dressing the consistency of thin mayonnaise. Season with salt and pepper and set aside.

On a plate mix paprika, cayenne and chili powder. Add chicken strips; toss until evenly coated in the mixture. In a skillet, heat vegetable oil over medium-low heat. Add coated chicken; stir-fry 2 to 3 minutes or until cooked though. Spoon chicken over the salad, then add salad dressing. Serve immediately.

Makes 4 servings.

CLUBHOUSE SALAD

2 thick slices white bread, crusts removed
Vegetable oil, for frying
12 ounces cooked chicken breast meat
6 ounces cooked smoked ham
6 ounces Swiss cheese
1 ripe avocado
2 hard-cooked eggs, shelled
5 tablespoons mayonnaise
1 tablespoon chopped fresh parsley
1/4 cup olive oil
1 tablespoon white-wine vinegar
1 teaspoon Dijon-style mustard
1 teaspoon sugar
Salt and pepper
Mixed salad greens
16 cherry tomatoes, halved

Cut bread into small cubes. In a skillet, heat 2 inches of oil. Add bread; fry until golden-brown. Remove with a slotted spoon. Drain on paper towels. Slice chicken into strips. Cut ham into 1-inch cubes. Cut Swiss cheese into strips. Cut avocado into bite-size pieces. Cut each egg into quarters. In a large bowl, mix together mayonnaise and parsley. Add chicken, ham, Swiss cheese, eggs and avocado; mix gently until all ingredients are well coated in mayonnaise.

In a small bowl, whisk together oil, vinegar, mustard, sugar, salt and pepper. Arrange greens, cherry tomatoes and croutons in a medium-size bowl. Pour dressing over salad and toss to combine. Arrange salad on a plate and spoon chicken mixture over salad.

Makes 4 servings.

—CHICKEN & SAFFRON SAUCE—

3 tablespoons chopped gingerroot
1 garlic clove, crushed
2 teaspoons each ground cumin and coriander
4 cardamom pods, cracked and seeds crushed
Finely grated peel and juice of 1/2 lemon
1/2 teaspoon curry powder
2/3 cup plain yogurt
4 boned and skinned chicken breast halves
Pinch of saffron strands
1 tablespoon hot water
1 shallot, finely chopped
1/4 cup dry white wine
2/3 cup chicken stock
1/3 cup whipping cream
1 tablespoon chopped fresh cilantro

In a food blender or food processor, process gingerroot, garlic, cumin, coriander, cardamom seeds, lemon peel and curry powder. Add two-thirds of the yogurt; mix well. Cut each chicken breast half into 8 strips. Put chicken into a shallow dish and top with yogurt mixture. Cover and refrigerate 1-1/2 to 2 hours. Meanwhile, soak saffron strands in hot water. Into a small pan, put shallot and wine. Boil rapidly until reduced by half. Add stock, saffron and water; boil until reduced to about 2/3 cup.

Add whipping cream. Simmer about 2 minutes or until sauce starts to thicken. Let cool, then stir in remaining yogurt. Season with a little lemon juice, salt and pepper. Preheat broiler. Remove chicken strips from marinade and place on a broiler pan, leaving space between strips to ensure even cooking. Broil 5 minutes or until browned, turning halfway through cooking. Arrange on a serving dish. Drizzle with sauce and sprinkle with cilantro.

Makes 4 servings.

-CHICKEN & HAM CROQUETTES-

1/4 cup butter or margarine
1 onion, finely chopped
1/2 cup all-purpose flour
1-1/4 cups milk
2-1/2 cups finely chopped cooked chicken
1/2 cup finely chopped ham
2 tablespoons chopped fresh parsley
1 teaspoon Dijon-style mustard
Salt and pepper
1-1/2 cups fresh white bread crumbs
Vegetable oil, for frying
Lemon wedges and green salad, to serve

In a saucepan, melt butter. Add onion; cook 3 to 4 minutes or until softened.

Add flour. Cook 1 minute, stirring. Gradually blend in milk and bring to a boil, stirring constantly. Reduce heat and simmer 2 minutes until sauce is a thick paste. Add chopped chicken, ham, parsley and mustard. Season with a little salt and pepper. Mix well and set aside to cool. Place bread crumbs on a plate. Drop tablespoons of chicken mixture onto bread crumbs.

Roll mixture in crumbs to give an even coating. Refrigerate 30 minutes. In a skillet, heat 2 tablespoons oil. Fry croquettes, a few at a time, until golden-brown. Drain on paper towels. Serve with lemon wedges and salad.

Makes 12 to 14 croquettes.

-HONEY CHICKEN DRUMSTICKS-

8 chicken drumsticks
1/4 cup honey
2 teaspoons Dijon-style mustard
2 teaspoons whole-grain mustard
1 teaspoon soy sauce
1 teaspoon dried rosemary
4 tablespoons mayonnaise (optional)
Lemon juice to taste (optional)

With a sharp knife, cut 3 diagonal slashes in flesh on both sides of drumsticks. Place drumsticks into a shallow baking dish or roasting pan.

In a small bowl, mix together honey, mustards and soy sauce. Pour over drumsticks. Cover and marinate 1 hour, turning occasionally.

Preheat oven to 400F (205C). Sprinkle rosemary over drumsticks. Roast 25 minutes. Increase heat to 450F (230C) and cook 10 minutes longer, basting and turning the drumsticks several times. If desired, any juices from pan can be added to the mayonnaise with a squeeze of lemon juice to make a sauce to serve with drumsticks.

Makes 4 servings.

—CHEESE & PEAR MUFFINS—

4 English muffins
1/4 cup garlic-and-herb-flavored butter
2 small cooked chicken breast halves
3 ounces dolcelatte cheese
1 small pear, sliced
Freshly ground pepper
Watercress sprigs, to garnish

Preheat broiler. Split muffins in half. Place on a baking sheet; broil until lightly browned on both sides.

Spread split side with a little flavored butter. With a sharp knife, cut chicken and cheese into thin slices. Arrange alternate pieces of chicken, cheese and pear on top of each muffin half.

Sprinkle with pepper. Return to broiler until cheese has melted. Serve at once, garnished with watercress sprigs.

Makes 4 servings.

—CHICKEN & SCRAMBLED EGG—

4 ounces cooked smoked chicken
1/4 cup butter or margarine
6 large eggs
2 tablespoons whipping cream
Juice of 1/2 lemon
Salt and pepper
4 thick slices brioche
2 tablespoons snipped fresh chives

With a sharp knife, cut chicken into match-stick strips. In a nonstick pan, melt butter. Add chicken strips and cook 1 minute.

In a bowl, beat eggs with 1 tablespoon cream and half the lemon juice. Season well with pepper. Pour over chicken in pan. Cook over very low heat, stirring constantly, until egg thickens. Remove from heat when eggs are almost fully cooked, but still creamy. Stir in remaining cream and lemon juice and season to taste with salt.

Preheat broiler. Broil brioche until lightly toasted. Place a brioche slice on each of 4 warmed serving plates. Top with generous spoonfuls of scrambled eggs. Sprinkle with chives and freshly ground pepper and serve at once.

Makes 4 servings.

——CHICKEN & HAM CREPES——

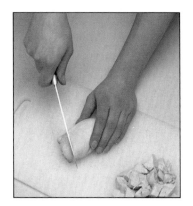

1 small onion, quartered
2-1/2 cups milk
1 bay leaf
2 tablespoons butter or margarine
1-1/4 cups all-purpose flour
3/4 cup (3 oz.) shredded Cheddar cheese
2 cups diced cooked chicken
1/2 pound broccoli flowerets, cooked until tender
8 thin ham slices
CREPES:
1 egg
1 cup milk
1/4 cup beer
Salt and pepper
Vegetable oil, for frying

In a small saucepan, combine onion, milk and bay leaf. Bring to a boil, then reduce heat and simmer 10 to 15 minutes until the onion softens. Discard bay leaf. In a blender or food processor, process onion mixture until pureed. In a pan, melt butter. Stir in 1/4 cup of the flour and cook 1 minute. Gradually stir in pureed mixture. Bring to a boil.

Remove pan from heat. Into a bowl, pour half the sauce. Stir in 1/2 cup of the cheese. Add chicken and broccoli to remaining sauce in pan. Return to heat to warm through.

Meanwhile, make crepes: In a blender or food processor, blend together flour, milk, beer, salt and pepper into a creamy batter. Heat a 6-inch crepe pan. Brush with a very little oil and pour in 2 to 3 tablespoons batter, tilting pan to cover bottom with a thin layer. Cook until top is opaque, then flip crepe over and cook the other side. Place in a warm oven. Repeat with remaining batter to make 8 crepes.

Preheat broiler. Butter a flameproof baking dish. Lay a slice of ham on each crepe and top with a generous spoonful of chicken mixture. Roll up each crepe to enclose filling. Place, fold-side down, in buttered dish.

Spoon reserved cheese sauce over crepes and sprinkle remaining cheese on top. Broil until golden and bubbly.

Makes 4 servings.

—HERBED CHICKEN FRITTATA—

2 tablespoons olive oil
2 large onions, thinly sliced
6 ounces waxy potatoes
5 jumbo eggs
3/4 cup (3 oz.) shredded sharp Cheddar cheese
2 tablespoons finely chopped fresh parsley
Salt and pepper
2 tablespoons butter or margarine
1-1/2 cups diced cooked chicken
Parsley sprigs, to garnish

In a skillet, heat oil. Add onions; cook, stirring occasionally, about 20 minutes or until golden brown. Cool slightly. Cook potatoes in boiling salted water until just tender.

Drain potatoes and cut into bite-size pieces. In a bowl, beat together eggs, cooked onions, cheese and parsley. Season with salt and pepper. In a skillet with a flameproof handle, melt butter. Stir in chicken. Pour in egg mixture, then stir in potatoes. Cook over low heat until the bottom sets and the top is runny. Preheat broiler.

Broil frittata until top is golden and bubbly. Cut into wedges; serve hot. Garnish with parsley sprigs.

Makes 4 servings.

ORIENTAL FRIED RICE

1-1/4 cups long-grain rice
1-1/4 cups chicken stock
2 tablespoons sesame oil
1 (1/2-inch) piece gingerroot, grated
1 garlic clove, crushed
6 ounces raw chicken, thinly sliced
6 green onions, sliced
1 small red bell pepper, sliced
4 ounces shelled shrimp
2 large eggs
2 tablespoons light soy sauce
1 tablespoon chopped fresh cilantro
1/3 cup cashew nuts, toasted

Into a saucepan, put rice and stock. Bring to a boil. Cover and simmer 10 minutes. Remove pan from heat and let stand 10 minutes longer. Drain off any excess liquid and cool slightly. In a large skillet or wok, heat sesame oil. Add gingerroot, garlic and chicken; stir-fry 4 to 5 minutes or until chicken is cooked.

Add onions, bell pepper and shrimp; stir-fry 1 minute longer. In a bowl, beat together eggs and soy sauce. Stir in rice. Continue to cook over high heat 1 minute, stirring. Remove from heat and stir in cilantro. Garnish with cashew nuts.

Makes 4 servings.

──── CHICKEN STIR-FRY ────

12 ounces skinned and boned chicken breast halves
2 tablespoons soy sauce
3 tablespoons dry sherry
3 tablespoons vegetable oil
1 garlic clove, finely chopped
1 (1-inch) piece gingerroot, chopped
1 small red bell pepper, sliced
4 green onions, cut into 1-inch pieces
2 ounces snow peas
8 baby corn, cut into halves lengthwise
1 teaspoon cornstarch
Few drops of sesame oil
Few drops of lemon juice

With a sharp knife, cut chicken breast into thin strips. Place chicken into a bowl. Add 1 teaspoon soy sauce and 1 tablespoon sherry. Marinate 35 minutes. In a wok or large skillet, heat oil over high heat. Add garlic and gingerroot and stir-fry 15 seconds. Add chicken and stir-fry 2 to 3 minutes. Add bell pepper, snow peas and baby corn and stir-fry 1 minute longer.

In a bowl, mix together cornstarch with remaining soy sauce and sherry. Pour into wok and cook 30 seconds until the sauce thickens and glazes all ingredients. Just before serving, drizzle with sesame oil and lemon.

Makes 4 servings.

COQ AU VIN

2-1/2 cups dry red wine
3 garlic cloves, sliced
1 small onion, chopped
2 tablespoons olive oil
1 teaspoon brown sugar
1 teaspoon mixed peppercorns, crushed
1 teaspoon coriander seeds, crushed
1 bouquet garni
1 (3-1/4-lb.) chicken, cut into 8 pieces
3 tablespoons all-purpose flour, seasoned
4 bacon slices, diced
6 ounces pearl onions
6 ounces button mushrooms
2 cups chicken stock
2 tablespoons chopped parsley
Fried bread croutons, to garnish

In a bowl, mix together wine, garlic, onion, 1 tablespoon of the oil, the sugar, peppercorns and coriander. Add bouquet garni and chicken pieces. Cover and refrigerate 2 to 3 hours, turning regularly. Remove chicken from marinade, reserving marinade, and pat chicken dry with paper towels. Toss in seasoned flour. In a Dutch oven, heat remaining oil. Add bacon; fry until browned. Remove with a slotted spoon; set aside. Add chicken to pan; fry on all sides until browned. Set aside with bacon.

Add onions. Cook until browned, then add mushrooms and remaining flour. Cook, stirring, 1 minute. Slowly stir in stock and marinade; cook, stirring, until thickened. Return chicken and bacon to pan. Cover and simmer 40 minutes. Transfer chicken and vegetables to a serving dish. Keep warm. Boil sauce until thickened. Taste for salt and stir in parsley. Spoon sauce over chicken. Garnish with croutons.

Makes 4 servings.

–CHICKEN VEGETABLE HOTPOT–

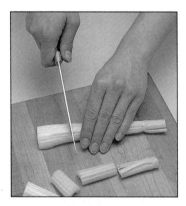

1/4 cup butter
4 bacon slices, chopped
2 large chicken quarters, halved
2 carrots, sliced
1 onion, sliced
2 celery stalks, cut into 2-inch pieces
2 leeks, sliced
2 tablespoons all-purpose flour
2 pounds potatoes, peeled
2 tablespoons chopped fresh thyme
2 tablespoons chopped fresh parsley
Salt and pepper
2 cups chicken stock

Preheat oven to 300F (150C). In a skillet, melt half of the butter. Add bacon and chicken and fry until golden. Remove from pan and drain on paper towels to remove excess fat. Add carrots, onion, celery and leeks to pan. Fry 2 to 3 minutes until vegetables are turning golden. Sprinkle flour over vegetables and mix well.

Slice potatoes into 1/4-inch-thick slices. Arrange half the slices in the bottom of a Dutch oven. Add chicken and bacon. Cover with vegetables and chopped herbs and season with salt and pepper. Cover with remaining sliced potatoes, dot with remaining butter and add stock. Cover and bake 1 hour, then uncover and bake 25 to 30 minutes longer until the chicken is tender and cooked through and potatoes are crisp and brown.

Makes 4 servings.

—CHICKEN IN CAPER SAUCE—

1 onion, quartered, and 1 carrot, quartered
1 teaspoon finely grated orange peel
1 orange, peeled and sliced
4 bay leaves
1/4 cup dry white wine
1 cup chicken stock
4 skinned and boned chicken breast halves
2 tablespoons butter or margarine
1/4 cup all-purpose flour
2/3 cup half and half
1 tablespoon chopped fresh parsley
2 teaspoons capers, drained
Salt and pepper

Put onion, carrot, orange peel, orange and bay leaves into a skillet.

Add wine and stock. Bring to a boil. Add chicken, reduce heat to a simmer, then cover and poach 20 minutes or until cooked through. Remove chicken, drain well on paper towels and keep warm. Strain and reserve poaching liquid.

In a pan, melt butter. Stir in flour; cook, stirring, 1 minute, remove from heat and slowly stir in poaching liquid, stirring well between each addition. Return to heat and bring to a boil, stirring constantly, until thickened. Stir in half and half, parsley and capers; season with salt and pepper. Spoon sauce over chicken. Serve with wild rice.

Makes 4 servings.

Note: Garnish with orange peel and parsley, if desired.

LEMON CHICKEN

1 egg white
12 ounces chicken breasts, sliced
3 teaspoons cornstarch
Finely grated peel and juice of 1 lemon
2 tablespoons dry sherry
1 teaspoon soy sauce
2 teaspoons honey
3 tablespoons vegetable oil
4 green onions, sliced
2 ounces snow peas, topped and tailed
1/2 red bell pepper, finely sliced
2 ounces bean sprouts

In a bowl, beat egg white until frothy. Add chicken and 2 teaspoons of the cornstarch.

Mix well. Mix in lemon peel. In a small bowl, mix together remaining cornstarch, sherry, lemon juice, soy sauce and honey. Set aside. In a wok or large skillet, heat oil. Add chicken pieces, a few at a time to prevent them from sticking together. Stir-fry 2 minutes or until chicken is cooked through.

Add green onions, snow peas, bell pepper and bean sprouts; stir-fry 1 minute longer. Add lemon juice and cornstarch mixture. Stir-fry 1 to 2 minutes, stirring until the sauce thickens and coats chicken and vegetables.

Makes 4 servings.

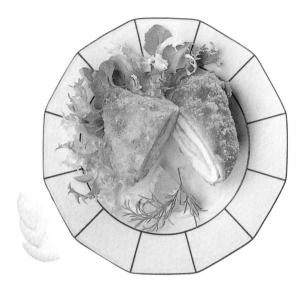

──CHICKEN CORDON BLEU──

4 skinned and boned chicken breast halves
4 ounces Swiss cheese
4 slices smoked ham
2 eggs, beaten
3 cups fresh white bread crumbs
Vegetable oil, for deep-frying

Lay chicken breasts between 2 sheets of waxed paper; pound to about 1/4 inch thick, taking care not to tear flesh. Trim ham slices so they are smaller than chicken breasts. Lay a slice on top of each breast half.

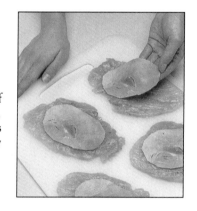

Cut cheese into very thin slices. Place on top of ham. Fold chicken breast in half to enclose filling. Carefully dip each chicken breast first in beaten egg, then into bread crumbs. Repeat until chicken is well coated and filling is completely enclosed.

Pour about 3 inches of oil into a deep pan. Heat to 375F (190C) or until an 1-inch bread cube browns in 40 seconds. Add chicken; fry 7 minutes, then decrease the heat and fry 5 minutes longer to ensure coating does not burn before chicken is cooked. Remove from oil with a slotted spoon. Drain well on paper towels. Serve hot.

Makes 4 servings.

——— CHICKEN KIEV ———

1/2 cup unsalted butter, softened
3 garlic cloves, crushed
Finely grated peel of 1/2 lemon
1 tablespoon chopped fresh parsley
Salt and pepper
4 skinned and boned chicken breast halves
2 eggs, beaten
3 cups fresh white bread crumbs
Vegetable oil, for deep frying

In a bowl, beat together butter, garlic, lemon peel, parsley, salt and pepper. Transfer to a pastry bag fitted with a plain 1/4-inch tip.

On a cutting board, lay chicken breasts. Insert a sharp knife into breast to form a pocket. Pipe butter into pocket; do not overfill or butter will burst through flesh. Refrigerate 25 minutes.

Dip a filled chicken breast half into beaten eggs, then roll in bread crumbs. Repeat, making sure chicken is well coated. Repeat with remaining chicken. Half-fill a deep-fryer or pan with oil. Heat to 375F (190C) or until an 1-inch bread cube browns in 40 seconds. Add chicken, 2 pieces at a time, and fry 8 to 10 minutes or until the chicken is cooked through and golden-brown. Drain on paper towels. Serve immediately with a squeeze of lemon juice.

Makes 4 servings.

— BROILED CHICKEN & HERBS —

4 chicken breast halves
2 garlic cloves, sliced
4 sprigs rosemary
6 tablespoons olive oil
Grated peel of 1/2 lemon
2 tablespoons dry white wine
Salt and pepper
1/2 teaspoon Dijon-style mustard
2 tablespoons balsamic vinegar
1 teaspoon sugar

With a sharp knife, make several incisions in chicken. Insert pieces of garlic and rosemary. Place chicken in a flameproof dish.

In a bowl, mix together 2 tablespoons olive oil with lemon peel and juice, wine, salt and pepper. Pour over chicken breast halves and marinate 45 minutes. Preheat broiler.

Place chicken breast halves, skin-sides down in dish. Broil 5 minutes. Turn chicken over and spoon marinade over chicken; broil 10 minutes longer or until skin is crisp and brown. Beat together mustard, vinegar, sugar, salt and pepper and remaining oil. Add any cooking juices from pan and spoon over chicken to serve.

Makes 4 servings.

— TANDOORI CHICKEN —

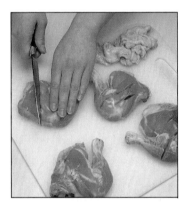

4 chicken leg quarters, skinned
Juice of 1 lemon
Salt
2 teaspoons ground turmeric
2 teaspoons paprika
1 teaspoon curry powder
1 teaspoon ground cardamom
1/2 teaspoon chili powder
Pinch of saffron powder
2 garlic cloves, crushed
2 teaspoons chopped gingerroot
1 tablespoon olive oil
3/4 cup plain yogurt
Lemon wedges, parsley and salsa, to garnish

Cut deep diagonal cuts in flesh.

Sprinkle chicken with lemon juice and a little salt. In a bowl, mix together remaining ingredients. Use to coat chicken quarters, cover and refrigerate 4 hours or overnight.

Preheat broiler. Cook chicken 25 minutes, brushing with any excess marinade and turning frequently until the chicken is tender and juices run clear when chicken leg is pierced with a knife. A slight blackening of the chicken gives an authentic look. Garnish with lemon wedges, parsley and salsa.

Makes 4 servings.

──── CORNISH GAME HENS ────

2 Cornish game hens
1/3 cup butter or margarine, softened
4 teaspoons chopped fresh rosemary
4 teaspoons chopped fresh basil
8 sun-dried tomatoes in oil, drained and chopped
Finely grated peel and juice of 1 lime
Salt and pepper

Prepare game hens. Using kitchen scissors, cut along backbone of each hen. Turn hen over so breast is facing up; flatten birds out by pressing down gently on breast.

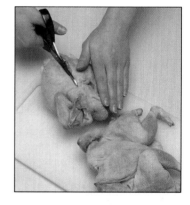

Running a sharp knife under skins, gently loosen skin on breast (starting at pointed end) taking care not to tear skin or cut flesh. Skin should not be separate but loosened enough to form a pocket in which to put butter. In a bowl, beat butter with a fork until soft. Add rosemary, basil, sun-dried tomatoes, lime peel and juice, salt and pepper.

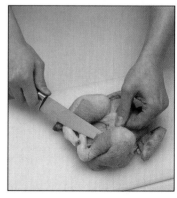

Preheat broiler. Using a table knife, spread butter mixture onto flesh under skin, making sure breast is well covered. Place game hens, breast-sides down, on a broiler pan. Cook under a very hot broiler 10 minutes until brown and crispy. Turn game hens over and broil 10 minutes longer until skins turn dark and crispy, spooning over any melted butter in pan. Serve immediately with boiled new potatoes and a green salad. Spoon over any melted butter left in broiler pan.

Makes 2 servings.

HASH CAKES

12 ounces cooked chicken, ground
8 green onions, chopped
1 pound potatoes, boiled and mashed
2 tablespoons mayonnaise
2 tablespoons chopped fresh parsley
1/2 teaspoon finely grated lemon peel
1/4 teaspoon freshly grated nutmeg
Salt and pepper
2 large eggs
1 cup fresh white bread crumbs
Vegetable oil, for frying

In a bowl, mix together chicken, onions, potatoes, mayonnaise, parsley, lemon peel, nutmeg, salt, pepper and 1 egg. Form into 8 cakes. Beat remaining egg. Dip cakes into egg, then coat in bread crumbs. Refrigerate 20 minutes.

In a large skillet, heat oil. Cook cakes on both sides 5 to 6 minutes or until golden. Drain well on paper towels. Serve hot with a green salad.

Makes 4 servings.

MINTED MEATBALLS

1 small onion, quartered
1 (14-oz.) can chopped tomatoes
1-1/4 cups chicken stock
Grated peel and juice of 1/2 large orange
2 tablespoons tomato paste
4 tablespoons chopped fresh mint
1 teaspoon sugar
1 teaspoon red-wine vinegar
1 pound raw chicken, ground
8 green onions, finely chopped
1 cup fresh white bread crumbs
1 small egg, beaten
2 teaspoons ground cumin
Salt and pepper
Vegetable oil, for frying

Into a blender or food processor, place onion, tomatoes, stock, orange peel and juice, tomato paste, 2 tablespoons of the chopped mint, the sugar and vinegar. Blend until smooth. Pour into a saucepan and simmer 10 to 15 minutes. In a large bowl, combine chicken with green onions, bread crumbs, egg, remaining mint, cumin, salt and pepper. Shape into 40 small meatballs. In a large nonstick pan, heat a little oil. Add meatballs; fry 6 to 8 minutes or until slightly browned all over. Remove from pan and drain on paper towels.

Wipe out skillet with paper towels. Return meatballs to skillet. Spoon sauce over meatballs and simmer, uncovered, 15 minutes. Serve on a bed of freshly cooked spaghetti, sprinkle with Parmesan cheese and garnish with mint sprigs.

Makes 4 servings.

PIQUANT MEAT LOAF

2 tablespoons butter or margarine
1 onion, finely chopped
1 garlic clove, crushed
3 ounces mushrooms, coarsely chopped
1/4 cup all-purpose flour
1-1/4 cups milk
1 cup fresh white bread crumbs
2 eggs, beaten
Finely grated peel and juice of 1 lemon
1 pound skinned and boned chicken breasts
2 bacon slices
1/3 cup chopped dried apricots
1 tablespoon chopped fresh thyme
2 tablespoons chopped fresh parsley
1/4 teaspoon grated nutmeg
Salt and pepper and thyme sprigs

Preheat oven to 400F (205C). In a pan, melt butter. Add onion and garlic; cook 2 to 3 minutes until softened but not browned. Add mushrooms and cook 1 minute longer. Add flour and cook, stirring, until all fat has been absorbed. Remove pan from heat and gradually stir in milk. Return pan to heat and simmer, stirring constantly, until sauce thickens. Add the bread crumbs. Transfer to a bowl and cool. Beat in the eggs and lemon juice.

In a food processor, finely process chicken breast and bacon. Transfer to a bowl. Add apricots, herbs, nutmeg, and lemon peel. Mix well. Add cooled sauce to chicken and bacon mixture and mix well. Season with salt and pepper. Transfer to a 9" × 5" loaf pan. Cover meat loaf with foil. Put into a roasting pan half-filled with hot water. Bake 55 to 60 minutes or until the loaf is firm. Serve hot or cold. Garnish with thyme.

Makes 4 servings.

CHICKEN BURGERS

3 ounces stuffing mix
1/2 pound ground chicken
1 small egg, beaten
1 apple, peeled, cored and grated
Salt and pepper
1 to 2 tablespoons vegetable oil
4 sesame seed buns
Iceberg lettuce, shredded
2 tomatoes, sliced
4 processed Cheddar cheese slices
Mayonnaise and relish, to serve

In a bowl, prepare stuffing mix according to package directions.

In a bowl, mix together chicken, stuffing, egg, apple, salt and pepper. Shape into 4 burgers. In a skillet, heat oil. Add burgers; cook 6 to 7 minutes on each side until cooked through.

Split buns in half. Cover bottoms with shredded lettuce and tomato slices. Cover each burger with a cheese slice and place over lettuce and tomato. Top with relish or mayonnaise. Place bun top in position.

Makes 4 servings.

— FRIED SHREDDED CHICKEN —

1 egg white
1 tablespoon cornstarch
Salt and pepper
12 ounces chicken breast, cut into thin strips
Vegetable oil, for frying
1 (1-inch) cube gingerroot, finely chopped
2 garlic cloves, sliced
1 large carrot, cut into matchstick strips
2 teaspoons sesame seeds
2 red chiles, seeded and thinly sliced
SAUCE:
2 teaspoons cornstarch
1/4 cup chicken stock
1 teaspoon each chili sauce, tomato paste and honey
1 tablespoon each dark soy sauce and dry sherry

In a bowl, beat egg white with cornstarch. Season chicken strips and coat in the egg white mixture. In a deep skillet or wok, heat oil. Fry chicken, a few strips at a time, 2 to 3 minutes until golden and crisp. Drain on paper towels while frying remainder. Pour all but 1 tablespoon oil out of pan. Add gingerroot, garlic, carrot, sesame seeds and chiles; stir-fry 2 to 3 minutes without browning.

Blend together all sauce ingredients. Pour over vegetables. Bring to a boil and cook, stirring, until thick and glossy. Add chicken, stir well to coat in the sauce and cook 1 to 2 minutes longer. Serve with fried rice and garnish with chives.

Makes 4 servings.

——— TOSTADAS WITH SALSA ———

8 corn or wheat tortillas, fried until crisp
1 (7-oz.) can refried beans
1 avocado, sliced
2 cooked chicken breast halves, sliced
1/2 cup dairy sour cream
4 small tomatoes, sliced
1 red onion, sliced
1 cup (4-oz.) shredded Cheddar cheese
SALSA:
4 green onions
1 (7-oz.) can chopped tomatoes
Hot pepper sauce to taste
1 teaspoon each tomato paste, sugar and red-wine
    vinegar
1 tablespoon chopped fresh cilantro

Preheat broiler. On a broiler pan, arrange tortillas. Warm refried beans and divide equally among tortillas. Top with sliced avocado, chicken, sour cream, tomatoes and onion. Sprinkle with cheese. Cook under a hot broiler until the cheese begins to melt.

Make Salsa: In a blender or food processor, blend together all Salsa ingredients 15 to 20 seconds. Serve with the tostadas.

Makes 4 servings.

——— JAMBALAYA ———

1 tablespoon olive oil
1 tablespoon butter or margarine
12 ounces skinned and boned chicken
6 ounces andouille or chorizo sausage
1 onion, thinly sliced
2 garlic cloves, sliced
1 red bell pepper, sliced
1 yellow bell pepper, sliced
1 green bell pepper, sliced
4 ounces mushrooms, sliced
1 cup long-grain white rice
1/2 teaspoon ground allspice
1-1/4 cups chicken stock
2/3 cup white wine
4 ounces shelled jumbo shrimp
Lime wedges and parsley, to garnish

In a large skillet, heat oil and butter. Cut chicken into thick strips. Fry until well browned, then remove from pan and set aside. Cut sausage into chunks. Fry 1 minute, stirring well, then, using a slotted spoon, add to chicken. Add onion and garlic; cook until slightly softened. Stir in bell peppers, mushrooms, rice and allspice. Cook, stirring, 1 minute longer.

Pour in stock and wine. Bring to a boil. Return chicken and sausage to pan and simmer, uncovered, 15 to 20 minutes until the liquid is absorbed and rice is tender. Stir in shrimp. Cook 5 minutes longer, then season to taste. Garnish with lime wedges and parsley.

Makes 4 servings.

SPICY FRIED CHICKEN

4 chicken breasts
Salt and pepper
3 tablespoons paprika
2 tablespoons ground coriander
1 tablespoon ground cumin
Finely grated peel and juice of 1 lemon
3 tablespoons dark soy sauce
2 tablespoons chopped fresh cilantro
1 teaspoon chopped fresh thyme
1 onion, finely chopped
2 garlic cloves, crushed
1 red chile, seeded and chopped
Vegetable oil, for frying
3/4 cup all-purpose flour
Lemon wedges, to garnish

Remove skin from chicken. Into a shallow dish, place chicken. Make several incisions in chicken pieces. Season well with salt and pepper. In a small bowl, mix together 2 tablespoons of the paprika, 1 tablespoon of the coriander and 2 teaspoons of the cumin. Sprinkle over chicken. In a small bowl, mix lemon peel and juice with soy sauce. Stir in cilantro, thyme, onion, garlic and chile. Pour over chicken, making sure chicken is well covered. Cover dish with plastic wrap and refrigerate 3 hours or overnight.

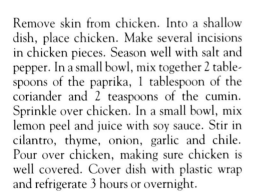

Half-fill a deep-fryer or pan with oil. Heat to 375F (190C) or until an 1-inch bread cube browns in 40 seconds. Put flour on a plate; season with salt and pepper. Add remaining paprika, cumin and coriander; mix well. Dip chicken pieces in flour to coat. Deep-fry chicken 15 minutes or until golden-brown and cooked through. Garnish with lemon wedges.

Makes 8 servings.

– GREEN-CHILE CHICKEN TACOS –

2 tablespoons vegetable oil
1 pound skinned and boned chicken breasts, cubed
8 green onions, chopped into 1-inch pieces
1 green bell pepper, chopped
1 garlic clove, crushed
2 fresh green chiles, finely chopped
1 teaspoon each chopped fresh basil and oregano
1 (14-oz.) can chopped tomatoes
1 (7-oz.) can red kidney beans, drained
2 teaspoons chili sauce
2 teaspoons tomato paste
1 teaspoon sugar
Salt and pepper
8 taco shells
1 head iceburg lettuce, shredded, and ripe olives, sliced
2/3 cup dairy sour cream

In a large skillet, heat oil. Add chicken; cook 2 to 3 minutes. Add green onions, bell pepper, garlic, chiles and herbs. Cook 2 minutes longer. Add tomatoes, kidney beans, chili sauce, tomato paste, sugar, salt and pepper. Simmer 20 to 25 minutes or until the sauce starts to thicken.

Spoon some chicken mixture into each taco shell. Top with lettuce, olives and a little sour cream.

Makes 4 servings.

CHICKEN FAJITAS

1/4 cup dry white wine
Finely grated peel and juice of 2 limes
1 tablespoon Worcestershire sauce
2 teaspoons brown sugar
1/2 teaspoon dried leaf basil
1/2 teaspoon dried leaf oregano
1 garlic clove, crushed
4 skinned and boned chicken breast halves
2 tablespoons vegetable oil
8 green onions, sliced
1 red bell pepper, sliced
1 green bell pepper, sliced
8 flour tortillas, warmed
2/3 cup dairy sour cream
Avocado, chopped
Oregano sprigs, to garnish

First prepare marinade for chicken. In a bowl, mix together wine, lime peel and juice, Worcestershire sauce, sugar, basil, oregano and garlic. Slice chicken breast into thin strips. Add to marinade. Mix well and marinate 30 to 40 minutes, stirring occasionally. In a skillet, heat 1 tablespoon of the oil. Add green onions and bell peppers; cook until onions are starting to brown, but the vegetables are still crisp. Remove from skillet and set aside. Drain chicken, reserving marinade.

In a skillet, heat remaining oil over medium-high heat. Add chicken (in several batches, if necessary) and fry quickly until golden-brown. Remove from pan with a slotted spoon and set aside. Add reserved marinade to pan and boil until thickened. Return chicken and peppers to skillet; mix well until all ingredients are coated. Put tortillas on a plate. Place spoonfuls of chicken mixture in middle of each tortilla; top with sour cream and avocado. Fold, garnish and serve.

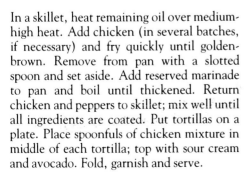

Makes 4 servings.

—CHICKEN & CORN FRITTERS—

1 ripe banana
1 egg
3/4 cup finely chopped cooked chicken
1 (8-oz.) can whole-kernel corn, drained
2 green onions, finely chopped
1/2 teaspoon ground cumin
2 teaspoons chopped fresh cilantro
Salt and red (cayenne) pepper
3/4 cup self-rising flour
Vegetable oil, for frying
Chili sauce or chutney
Cilantro, to garnish

Mash the banana in a bowl. Add egg, chicken, corn and green onions.

Stir in cumin, cilantro, salt and cayenne. Mix well. Add flour and mix to form a soft batter. In a heavy-bottomed skillet, heat oil. Add spoonfuls of chicken mixture. Cook about 1 minute, turning once.

Remove fritters from pan with a slotted spoon. Drain well on paper towels. Serve fritters warm with a chili sauce or chutney. Garnish with cilantro.

Makes 4 servings.

GUMBO

2 tablespoons butter or margarine
1 tablespoon vegetable oil
1 (3-lb.) chicken, cut into 8 pieces
1/4 cup all-purpose flour, seasoned with salt and pepper
1 large onion, sliced
2 garlic cloves, sliced
2 teaspoons chili powder
1 (14-oz.) can chopped tomatoes
2 tablespoons tomato paste
1-1/4 cups chicken stock
1/2 cup red wine
1 red bell pepper, sliced
1 green bell pepper, sliced
3/4 pound small okra, trimmed
2 teaspoons lemon juice
Pinch of sugar

Preheat oven 350F (175C). In a Dutch oven, heat butter and oil. Toss chicken pieces in seasoned flour. Add chicken to pan; cook until golden. Remove from pan and set aside. Add onion and garlic; cook until slightly softened. Stir in chili powder and any remaining flour, then add tomatoes, tomato paste, stock and wine. Bring to a boil.

Stir in vegetables, lemon juice and sugar. Return chicken to pan. Cover and cook in oven 50 to 60 minutes or until chicken juices run clear when pierced with a fork. Serve with rice, if desired.

Makes 4 servings.

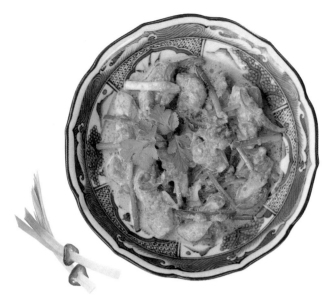

THAI CURRY

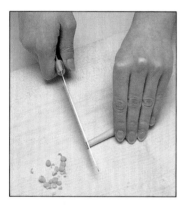

1 small onion, chopped
1 garlic clove, peeled
1 blade lemon grass, chopped
1 teaspoon ground coriander
1 teaspoon grated lime peel
1 teaspoon paprika
1/2 teaspoon ground cumin
1/2 teaspoon dried chile flakes
2 teaspoons vegetable oil
1 pound skinned and boned chicken, sliced
1 tablespoon light soy sauce
2/3 cup coconut milk
2 lime leaves
1/4 cup chicken stock
2 red bell peppers, sliced
10 green onions, sliced into matchstick strips

In a blender or food processor, process onion, garlic, lemon grass, coriander, peel, paprika, cumin and chile flakes until pureed. In a large skillet, heat oil. Stir in puree and cook 1 to 2 minutes. Add chicken. Stir gently, coating well in pureed mixture.

Stir in soy sauce, coconut milk, lime leaves, chicken stock, bell peppers and green onions. Cover and cook 20 to 25 minutes. Serve with plain boiled rice.

Makes 4 servings.

—— SWEET & SOUR CHICKEN ——

1-1/2 pounds skinned and boned chicken breasts
Salt
5 tablespoons cornstarch
2 cups self-rising flour
3 large eggs, beaten
1 (1-inch) piece gingerroot, finely chopped
1 tablespoon vegetable oil, plus extra for frying
1/2 cup white-wine vinegar
1/4 cup dry sherry
1/2 cup orange juice
3 tablespoons soy sauce
1/4 cup tomato paste
1 garlic clove, finely chopped
1 small onion, finely chopped
1 red bell pepper, sliced
1 green bell pepper, sliced

Cut chicken into 1-inch cubes. Sprinkle with salt and 2 tablespoons cornstarch; mix thoroughly. Meanwhile, make batter. Into a bowl put flour. Gradually add eggs and 1-1/4 cups water to make a smooth batter. Add half of the gingerroot. Add chicken cubes and coat thoroughly. Half-fill a deep pan or deep-fat fryer with oil. Heat to 375F (190C) or until an 1-inch bread cube browns in 40 seconds. Add chicken, in batches, and fry 4 to 5 minutes or until golden and crispy. Drain well on paper towels. Transfer to a plate to keep warm.

In a small bowl, mix remaining 3 tablespoons cornstarch with 2/3 cup water, then add vinegar, sherry, orange juice, soy sauce and tomato paste. In a wok or large skillet, heat the 1 tablespoon oil. Add garlic and remaining gingerroot. Stir-fry 15 seconds. Add onion and bell peppers and stir-fry 1-1/2 minutes. Stir in cornstarch mixture; cook, stirring, until thickened. Put chicken into a warm serving dish; top with vegetables and sauce.

Makes 4 to 6 servings.

─── CHICKEN CHOW MEIN ───

3 tablespoons dark soy sauce
2 tablespoons dry sherry
1 teaspoon brown sugar
1 teaspoon sweet chili sauce
1/2 pound skinned and boned chicken, shredded
1/2 pound egg thread noodles
1 teaspoon cornstarch
6 tablespoons chicken stock or water
3 tablespoons vegetable oil
1 (1-inch) piece gingerroot, finely chopped
1 garlic clove, finely chopped
4 green onions, sliced
1 cup (1-inch pieces) green beans
1 small carrot, cut into matchstick strips
1 red pepper, seeded and finely sliced
6 ounces bean sprouts

In a bowl, mix together soy sauce, sherry, brown sugar and chili sauce. Add chicken and marinate 30 minutes. Drain chicken, reserving marinade. Cook noodles according to package directions. Drain well and set aside. Mix reserved marinade with cornstarch and chicken stock. Set aside.

In a wok or large skillet, heat oil. Add gingerroot and garlic. Stir-fry 15 to 20 seconds, then add chicken and stir-fry 2 to 3 minutes longer until chicken is cooked. Add green onions, beans, carrot and pepper. Stir-fry 1 minute. Add noodles and bean sprouts. Stir-fry 30 seconds, then add marinade mixture and stir-fry until sauce thickens and coats ingredients. Serve immediately.

Makes 4 servings.

CHICKEN & BLACK BEAN SAUCE

1 teaspoon cornstarch
4 teaspoons light soy sauce
1 (1-inch) piece gingerroot, finely chopped
1 garlic clove, crushed
12 ounces skinned and boned chicken breasts
1 green bell pepper, seeded
8 canned water chestnuts, drained
4 green onions
2 tablespoons vegetable oil
1/2 cup cashews
5 tablespoons dry sherry
3/4 cup bottled black bean sauce

In a bowl, mix together cornstarch, soy sauce, gingerroot and garlic. Slice chicken into thin strips. Coat chicken strips in cornstarch mixture and let stand 10 minutes. Dice green pepper. Cut water chestnuts in half. Slice green onions into 1-inch pieces. Set aside.

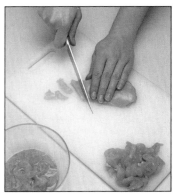

In a wok or large skillet, heat oil. Add chicken and stir-fry 2 minutes. Add bell pepper, green onions and water chestnuts and stir-fry 1 minute longer. Add cashews, sherry and black bean sauce. Stir-fry until sauce thickens.

Makes 4 servings.

ARABIAN POUSSINS

2 tablespoons olive oil
1 small red onion, finely chopped
1-1/4 cups couscous
1-1/2 cups chicken stock
1/4 cup finely chopped dried apricots
2 tablespoons raisins
Grated peel and juice of 1/2 lemon
1/4 cup pine nuts, toasted
1 tablespoon chopped fresh mint
4 poussins (young chickens)
Salt and pepper
2/3 cup dry white wine
2 teaspoons mint jelly
Mint sprigs, to garnish

Preheat oven to 350F (175C). In a pan, heat 1 tablespoon of the oil. Add onion; cook until softened. Put couscous into a bowl. Add 1 cup of the stock, the cooked onion, apricots, raisins and lemon peel and juice. Let stand 15 minutes. Stir in pine nuts and mint. Loosen skin around the breast of each poussin. Carefully push stuffing around meat, securing skin in place with a wooden pick. Place any excess stuffing under poussins in a roasting pan.

Brush poussins with remaining oil and sprinkle with salt and pepper. Roast 50 to 60 minutes, basting occasionally. Remove poussins from roasting pan and set aside. Pour remaining stock, the wine and mint jelly into pan and stir over high heat. Bring to a boil. Spoon over poussins and serve. Garnish with mint sprigs.

Makes 4 servings.

TIKKA KABOBS

2/3 cup plain yogurt
1 tablespoon grated gingerroot
2 garlic cloves, crushed
1 teaspoon chili powder
1 teaspoon ground cumin
1 teaspoon turmeric
1 tablespoon coriander seeds
Juice of 1 lemon
1/2 teaspoon salt
2 tablespoons chopped fresh cilantro
12 ounces skinned and boned chicken, cubed
RAITA:
2/3 cup plain yogurt
2 teaspoons mint jelly
3/4 cup finely chopped cucumber
2 green onions, finely chopped

In a blender or food processor, process yogurt, gingerroot, garlic, chili powder, cumin, turmeric, coriander seeds, lemon juice, salt and cilantro until smooth. Pour into a bowl. Stir in chicken, cover and refrigerate over-night.

Preheat broiler. Thread chicken cubes onto skewers. Broil 15 to 20 minutes, turning frequently and brushing with any remaining marinade. In a small bowl, mix together Raita ingredients. Serve kabobs on a bed of pilaf rice. Garnish with mint sprigs. Pass Raita separately.

Makes 4 servings.

CHICKEN BIRYANI

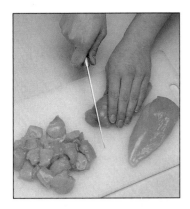

8 tablespoons vegetable oil
1 cinnamon stick
8 whole cloves
6 cardamom pods, bruised
1 (1-inch) piece gingerroot, finely chopped
1-1/2 pounds skinned and boned chicken, cubed
2 garlic cloves, crushed
1 teaspoon chili powder
1-1/4 cups plain yogurt
2/3 cup chicken stock
Pinch of saffron threads
1/4 cup boiling water
2-1/4 cups basmati rice
1/4 cup golden raisins
1/4 cup slivered almonds
1 onion, sliced

Preheat oven to 375F (190C). In a Dutch oven, heat 4 tablespoons of the oil. Add spices and fry 15 seconds. Add chicken, garlic and chili powder and fry, stirring, 4 minutes. Add yogurt, 1 tablespoon at a time, stirring between each addition until yogurt is absorbed by spices. Add stock and simmer 20 to 25 minutes. Transfer to a bowl. In a small bowl, soak saffron in boiling water and set aside. Rinse rice under cold running water until water runs clear. In a medium-size saucepan, cook rice in 5 cups boiling salted water 3 minutes, then drain, if necessary.

Wash Dutch oven. Add 2 tablespoons of the oil. Spoon in a layer of rice, sprinkle with a little saffron water and cover with a layer of chicken. Repeat, ending with a layer of rice. Add any cooking juices left from chicken, cover tightly and cook 25 to 30 minutes. In a small pan, heat remaining oil. Fry golden raisins and almonds until golden; remove. Add onion; fry until crisp and golden. Sprinkle biryani with almonds, onion and golden raisins.

Makes 4 servings.

CURRIED CHICKEN

6 garlic cloves
3/4 cup blanched almonds
1 (1-inch) piece gingerroot, chopped
6 tablespoons vegetable oil
2-1/4 pounds chicken pieces
9 whole cardamom pods
1 cinnamon stick
6 whole cloves
1 onion, finely chopped
2-1/2 teaspoons ground cumin
1 teaspoon red (cayenne) pepper
2/3 cup plain yogurt
1-1/4 cups whipping cream
1 firm, ripe banana
1 tablespoon golden raisins
1/2 teaspoon each curry powder and salt

In a blender or food processor, process garlic, almonds, gingerroot and 1/4 cup water until pureed. Cut chicken into bite-size pieces. In a Dutch oven, heat oil. Add chicken; cook, stirring, until golden. Set aside. Add cardamom, cinnamon and cloves to pan. Fry a few seconds. Add onion and fry until beginning to turn golden-brown. Add puree from blender or food processor together with cumin and cayenne. Cook, stirring, 2 minutes or until mixture is lightly browned.

Stir in 1 tablespoon of the yogurt. Cook about 20 seconds, then stir in another tablespoon. Cook about 20 seconds. Continue adding remaining yogurt this way. Add chicken and any juices and cream. Bring to a simmer, stirring. Cover pan and simmer about 20 minutes. Slice banana. Add raisins and sliced banana and cook 10 minutes longer or until the chicken is tender. Stir in the curry powder and salt.

Makes 4 servings.

CACCIATORE

2 tablespoons olive oil
4 large chicken breast halves
1 cup thinly sliced red onion
2 garlic cloves, thinly sliced
2/3 cup red wine
2/3 cup chicken stock
1 (14-oz.) can chopped tomatoes
1 tablespoon tomato paste
1 red bell pepper, sliced
1 yellow bell pepper, sliced
2 tablespoons chopped fresh basil
Salt and black pepper
Pinch of sugar
Pasta noodles, to serve

Preheat oven to 350F (175C). In a skillet, heat oil. Add chicken; cook, turning, until golden-brown, then transfer to a shallow casserole dish. Add onion and garlic to pan; cook over low heat until softened. Add wine, stock, tomatoes, tomato paste, bell peppers, 1 tablespoon of the basil, salt, black pepper and sugar. Bring to a boil.

Pour over chicken; cover. Bake 45 minutes or until chicken is tender. Serve on pasta noodles and sprinkle with the remaining basil and plenty of black pepper.

Makes 4 servings.

──── CHICKEN WITH APPLES ────

1 (3-1/4- to 3-1/2-lb.) chicken
Peel and 1 teaspoon juice from 1 lemon
1/2 cinnamon stick
1 onion, quartered
Salt and pepper
1/2 cup butter or margarine
1 tablespoon vegetable oil
3 tablespoons brandy
1 pound Golden Delicious apples
2/3 cup apple juice
1 cup half and half
1 tablespoon each chopped fresh chives and parsley

Place peel, cinnamon stick and onion in cavity of chicken. Season.

Preheat oven to 350F (175C). In a Dutch oven, melt 1/4 cup of the butter and the oil. Add chicken; brown on all sides. Add brandy and ignite. Peel and thinly slice 1 apple; add to pan when flames die down. Add apple juice; bring to a boil. Cover and cook 1-1/4 hours.

In a pan, melt remaining butter. Peel remaining apples; cut into thick slices. Add to butter; cook until just tender. Remove chicken from pan; place on a warmed platter. Surround with cooked apples. Add half and half to pan. Stir well and simmer to reduce slightly. Season well and pour over chicken. Sprinkle with chopped herbs and serve at once.

Makes 4 to 6 servings.

—CHICKEN & VEGETABLES—

1 tablespoon vegetable oil
4 bacon slices, chopped
2 garlic cloves
12 shallots
1 celery stalk, cut into 1-inch pieces
2 small turnips, quartered
2 carrots, cut into matchsticks
1/2 pound button mushrooms
2/3 cup dry white wine
2/3 cup chicken stock
1 (3-lb.) chicken
1/4 cup whipping cream
Juice of 1/2 lemon
Salt and pepper
Fresh rosemary, to garnish

Preheat oven to 400F (205C). In a Dutch oven, heat oil. Add bacon, garlic and shallots. Fry 2 to 3 minutes. Add remaining vegetables and fry 2 to 3 minutes longer until bacon starts to turn golden-brown. Pour wine over vegetables and boil rapidly to reduce liquid by half. Add chicken stock. Remove pan from heat and add chicken. Cover and bake 45 to 55 minutes.

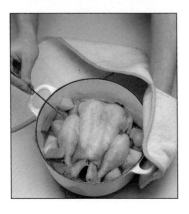

To check if chicken is cooked, pierce leg with a skewer. If juices do not run clear, cook a few minutes longer before testing again. When cooked, transfer chicken and vegetables to a serving dish. Cover and keep warm. Return pan to heat. Skim off any fat from cooking juices and boil until reduced to just over 2/3 cup. Add cream and simmer 2 minutes. Add lemon juice, salt and pepper. Serve hot with chicken.

Makes 4 servings.

CASSOULET

1-1/4 cups dried white beans, soaked overnight
3-1/4 cups chicken stock
2 tablespoons olive oil
8 chicken thighs
4 bacon slices, coarsely chopped
1 large onion, thinly sliced
2 garlic cloves, thinly sliced
2/3 cup dry white wine
1 (7-oz.) can chopped tomatoes
2 tablespoons tomato paste
1 bay leaf
Salt and pepper
1/2 pound kielbasa sausage, cut into large chunks
2 tablespoons butter or margarine
1 cup fresh white bread crumbs
2 tablespoons chopped fresh parsley

Drain beans. Into a large pan, put beans with 2-1/2 cups of the stock and enough water to cover. Boil 10 minutes, reduce heat and simmer 50 minutes. Preheat oven to 350F (175C). In a skillet, heat 1 tablespoon of the oil. Add chicken; cook until golden, turning. Remove from pan and set aside. Add bacon; fry until lightly browned, then add onion and garlic and cook until softened. Drain beans and return to pan with wine, remaining stock, tomatoes, tomato paste, bay leaf, salt and pepper. Bring to a boil. Stir in bacon mixture.

Transfer half the bean mixture into a Dutch oven. Arrange chicken thighs and sausage on top and cover with remaining beans. Cover and bring to a boil. Bake 1 hour. In a skillet, heat butter and remaining oil. Fry the bread crumbs until golden, then stir in parsley. Sprinkle bread crumbs over chicken. Cook, uncovered, 15 to 20 minutes longer. Discard bay leaf. Serve with crusty bread and a salad.

Makes 4 servings.

— MOROCCAN CHICKEN —

3 garlic cloves, crushed, or 1-2 tablespoons garlic paste
1 teaspoon paprika
1 teaspoon ground ginger
1/2 teaspoon ground cumin
4 tablespoons olive oil
4 skinned and boned chicken breast halves
1 large onion, finely chopped
4 tablespoons chopped fresh parsley
Pinch saffron threads
2/3 cup chicken stock
12 green olives
Finely grated peel and juice of 1/2 lemon
Salt and pepper

In a bowl, mix garlic, paprika, ginger and cumin with 3 tablespoons of the olive oil.

Place chicken into a shallow bowl. Pour oil mixture over chicken, cover and refrigerate 3 to 4 hours. In a skillet, heat remaining oil. Add onion and cook over low heat 2 to 3 minutes. Add chicken pieces and marinade to pan and brown chicken slightly. Add parsley, saffron and chicken stock. Cover and simmer 30 minutes or until the chicken is tender.

Remove chicken from pan and keep warm. Add olives, lemon peel and lemon juice. Season with a little salt and pepper. Bring to a boil and boil rapidly until reduced to about 2/3 cup. Pour sauce over chicken and serve immediately.

Makes 4 servings.

——— LENTIL-BAKED CHICKEN ———

1-1/4 cups green lentils
2 tablespoons butter or margarine
1 tablespoon olive oil
1 (3-1/4 to 3-1/2-lb.) chicken
6 bacon slices, coarsely chopped
12 shallots, halved
4 garlic cloves, thickly sliced
2/3 cup dry white wine
1-1/4 cups chicken stock
1 bouquet garni
Chopped fresh parsley, to garnish

Preheat oven 400F (205C). Add lentils to a large pan of lightly salted water. Bring to a boil, then simmer 15 minutes.

In a Dutch oven, heat butter and oil. Add chicken; cook, turning to brown on all sides, then remove from pan and set aside. Add bacon, shallots and garlic to pan. Cook 2 to 3 minutes. Drain lentils and stir into bacon mixture. Place chicken on lentils. Add wine, stock and bouquet garni. Bring to a boil. Cover and bake 50 minutes.

Add a little water if lentil mixture is too dry. Bake, uncovered, 35 to 40 minutes longer until chicken juices run clear when pierced. Remove bouquet garni and garnish with chopped fresh parsley.

Makes 4 to 6 servings.

CHICKEN POTPIE

1-1/2 pounds chicken pieces
1 large onion, thickly sliced
1/3 cup dry white wine
3/4 cup chicken stock
1 bouquet garni
2 tablespoons butter or margarine
2-1/2 cups halved button mushrooms
1/4 cup all-purpose flour
1 (8-oz.) whole-kernel corn, drained
2 tablespoons chopped fresh parsley
1 teaspoon fresh lemon juice
1/4 cup whipping cream
2 pounds potatoes
1/2 cup milk
3/4 cup shredded Cheddar cheese
1 ounce salted potato chips

In a large pan, place chicken, onion, wine, stock and bouquet garni. Bring to a boil. Reduce heat and simmer 25 to 30 minutes or until chicken is tender. Drain liquid; reserve liquid and onion. Discard bouquet garni. Remove skin and bones from chicken; coarsely chop flesh. In a pan, melt butter. Add mushrooms; cook until softened. Stir in flour; cook 1 minute. Add reserved liquid and onion.

Bring to a boil, stirring constantly. Stir in chicken, corn, parsley, lemon juice and cream. Season to taste with salt and pepper. Boil potatoes until tender. Drain and mash with milk and 1/2 cup of the cheese; season to taste. Preheat broiler. Cover casserole with potatoes. Crush potato chips and mix with remaining cheese. Sprinkle over potatoes. Broil until golden.

Makes 4 servings.

—CHICKEN & HAM POTPIE—

2 tablespoons butter or margarine
1/2 pound cooked ham, cut into 1-inch cubes
3/4 pound skinned and boned chicken, cut into 1-inch cubes
1 onion, chopped
1-1/3 cups sliced leeks
6 ounces button mushrooms
1/4 cup all-purpose flour
1-1/4 cups chicken stock
2/3 cup half and half
Finely grated peel of 1/2 lemon
Salt and pepper
1 prepared flat pie crust
Milk, for glazing
2 tablespoons grated Parmesan cheese

Preheat oven to 400F (205C). In a pan, melt butter, add ham and chicken and cook 2 to 3 minutes. Remove from pan and reserve. Add vegetables and cook 2 to 3 minutes or until softened. Return ham and chicken to pan. Stir in flour and cook 1 to 2 minutes. Remove from heat. Gradually stir in stock and half and half. Return to heat and cook, stirring, 2 minutes until thickened. Add lemon peel and season with salt and pepper.

Transfer chicken mixture to a deep 9-inch-round ovenproof dish. Cut off an 1-inch strip from pastry to fit edge of dish. Position dough strip on edge and brush with a little water. Cover with remaining pastry. Pinch edges together to seal. Brush pastry with milk to glaze. Sprinkle with cheese. Bake 25 minutes or until the pastry is golden-brown.

Makes 4 servings.

CHICKEN & MUSHROOM COBBLER

2 tablespoons butter or margarine
1 small onion, finely chopped
2-1/2 cups sliced mushrooms
1/4 cup all-purpose flour
3/4 cup chicken stock
3/4 cup half and half
4 cups diced cooked chicken
Salt and pepper
2 tablespoons chopped fresh parsley
BISCUIT DOUGH:
1 cup all-purpose flour
1/4 cup butter or margarine
1/4 cup shredded Cheddar cheese
3 tablespoons milk

Preheat oven to 375F (190C). In a large pan, melt butter. Add onion and mushrooms and cook 2 to 3 minutes until the vegetables start to soften. Sprinkle with flour; cook, stirring, 1 minute. Gradually blend in stock and half and half. Return pan to heat and cook 2 minutes, stirring, or until sauce thickens.

Add chicken. Season with salt and pepper; mix in parsley. Transfer to an ovenproof serving dish. Prepare Biscuit Dough: Into a bowl, sift flour. Cut in butter until mixture resembles crumbs, then stir in cheese. Stir in enough milk to form a soft but not sticky dough. On a floured surface, roll out dough 1 inch thick. With a fluted cutter, cut out 12 circles. Arrange circles, overlapping, around edge of dish; brush with milk. Bake 35 to 40 minutes or until golden. Serve hot.

Makes 4 servings.

——————CHICKEN & FETA PIE——————

2 cups ground cooked chicken
3/4 pound frozen spinach leaves, thawed, drained and
    chopped
6 ounces feta cheese
1 teaspoon finely grated lemon peel
2 teaspoons fresh lemon juice
1/4 teaspoon freshly grated nutmeg
Freshly ground pepper
6 sheets filo dough
3 tablespoons butter or margarine, melted

In a large bowl, mix together chicken, spinach, cheese, lemon peel, lemon juice, nutmeg and pepper.

Brush 1 sheet of filo dough with butter. Press it gently into an 11″ × 7″ nonstick pan, leaving ends of dough overlapping edges of pan. Repeat with a second sheet of dough, placed at a 90 degree angle; repeat with 2 more sheets of dough, brushing with butter each time.

Spoon spinach filling into crust. Bring overlapping dough over filling. Crumple remaining dough and arrange loosely on top of pie. Brush lightly with any remaining butter. Bake 25 to 30 minutes or until golden and crisp.

Makes 4 to 6 servings.

──────── CHICKEN PASTIES ────────

3 cups all-purpose flour
1/3 cup butter or margarine
1/3 cup vegetable shortening
1 tablespoon chopped fresh thyme
12 ounces chicken breasts, ground
1 tablespoon vegetable oil
2 bacon slices, chopped
1/2 onion, chopped
1 large potato, diced
1 carrot, diced
1 cup chopped mushrooms
1/2 tablespoon all-purpose flour
2/3 cup chicken stock
Beaten egg or milk, for brushing
Parsley and thyme sprigs, to garnish

Preheat oven to 375F (190C). Into a bowl, sift flour and a pinch of salt. Add butter and shortening; cut in until mixture resembles bread crumbs. Add chopped thyme and 3 tablespoons iced water. Mix together to form a dough. Wrap in plastic wrap; refrigerate 30 minutes. In a skillet, heat oil. Add bacon, onion, potato and carrot. Fry 2 to 3 minutes until onion starts to soften. Add chicken and mushrooms and cook, stirring, 3 to 4 minutes longer. Stir in flour; cook, stirring, 1 minute.

Gradually stir in stock. Return to heat and cook, stirring, until thickened. Season with salt and pepper; cool. On a floured surface, roll out dough. Cut out 8 (6-inch) circles. Place 2 tablespoons chicken mixture in center of each circle. Brush edges with beaten egg or milk and fold dough over to enclose filling. Pinch edges to seal. Glaze with egg or milk and place on a baking sheet. Bake 20 to 25 minutes or until golden.

Makes 4 servings.

— STUFFED CHICKEN PASTRIES —

4 skinned and boned chicken breast halves
4 ounces duck liver pate
1 teaspoon finely grated orange peel
1 tablespoon orange juice
5 fresh thyme sprigs
Salt and pepper
2 tablespoons butter or margarine
2 teaspoons olive oil
About 1-1/2 sheets puff pastry dough from a 17-1/2-oz. pkg.
1 large egg, beaten
1 teaspoon poppy seeds

Cut a small incision in each chicken breast to make a pocket.

Mix together pâté, orange peel, orange juice, 1 finely chopped thyme sprig, salt and pepper. Transfer mixture to a pastry bag fitted with a plain tip. Pipe one-quarter of the mixture into each pocket. Secure edges with a wooden pick. In a skillet, heat butter and oil. Add chicken; cook quickly on both sides until well browned. Remove from heat. Drain well and cool, then refrigerate until chilled. Preheat oven to 400F (205C). Thinly roll out dough and cut into 1-1/2-inch-wide strips. Discard wooden picks from chicken. Top each breast half with a thyme sprig.

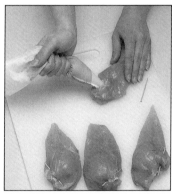

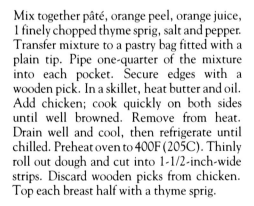

Brush dough strips with egg and wind strips, egg-side in, around breast halves, over-lapping very slightly to enclose chicken completely. On a lightly dampened baking sheet, place dough-covered chicken. Brush with remaining egg and sprinkle with poppy seeds. Make a small hole in top of each one. Bake 35 to 40 minutes or until golden. Serve with an orange salad.

Makes 4 servings.

PUFF PASTRY ROLLS

1 tablespoon vegetable oil
2 shallots, finely chopped
1 garlic clove, crushed
1-1/2 cups finely chopped mushrooms
1 tablespoon chopped fresh sage
1 tablespoon chopped fresh thyme
1/2 pound skinned and boned chicken meat
2 tablespoons plain yogurt
2 tablespoons grated Parmesan cheese
Salt and pepper
1 sheet puff pastry dough from a 17-1/4-oz. pkg.
1 egg, beaten

Preheat oven to 400F (205C). In a small pan, heat oil. Add shallots, garlic and mushrooms; fry 3 to 4 minutes until softened. Add chopped herbs and set aside to cool. Finely chop chicken. Transfer to a bowl and add yogurt, 1 tablespoon of the Parmesan cheese and the mushroom mixture. Season with a little salt and pepper; mix well. On a floured surface, roll out pastry dough to a 12″ × 16″ rectangle. Cut into 4 strips lengthwise.

Place spoonfuls of mixture along the length of each strip. Brush edges with a little beaten egg and fold dough over to enclose filling. Pinch edges of dough together to seal. Brush with a little more beaten egg and sprinkle with the remaining Parmesan cheese. Cut into 2-inch pieces and make 2 slashes in each roll. Place on a greased baking sheet. Bake 15 to 20 minutes or until golden-brown.

Makes 4 servings.

—CHICKEN & TOMATO POTPIE—

2 cups all-purpose flour
Pinch of salt
1/4 cup unsalted butter, diced
1/4 cup vegetable shortening, chilled and diced
2 tablespoons iced water
1 pound cooked chicken, skinned and boned
6 tomatoes, sliced
1-1/4 cups dairy sour cream
3 tablespoons pesto sauce
Salt and pepper
Beaten egg or milk for glazing

Preheat oven to 375F (190C). To make pastry, into a bowl, sift flour and salt. Add butter and shortening and cut in until mixture resembles bread crumbs. Add water and mix together until dough forms a ball. Wrap in plastic wrap and refrigerate 30 minutes. With a sharp knife, cut chicken into slices. Layer with tomatoes in an 8-inch ovenproof serving dish, filling almost to top. Mix together sour cream and pesto in a small bowl. Season with salt and pepper. Pour over chicken and tomatoes.

Roll out dough. Using the pie dish as a guide, cut out a piece slightly larger than dish. Brush with a little water. Arrange dough over filling. Pinch edge to crimp. Brush pie with a little beaten egg or milk to glaze. Bake 25 to 30 minutes or until pastry is golden and crisp. Serve hot or chilled.

Makes 4 servings.

─── ROQUEFORT VERONIQUE ───

2 tablespoons butter
1 tablespoon vegetable oil
4 skinned and boned chicken breast halves
1 leek, chopped
2 teaspoons all-purpose flour
3/4 cup milk
2-1/2 ounces Roquefort cheese
1/3 cup half and half
5 ounces seedless green grapes, halved
Chopped fresh parsley, to garnish

In a skillet, heat butter and oil. Add chicken; cook, turning, until golden on all sides.

Reduce heat. Stir in chopped leek. Cover and cook 30 minutes or until chicken juices run clear when chicken is pierced. Remove chicken from skillet; set aside on a warmed plate.

Sprinkle flour into pan; cook, stirring, 1 minute. Remove from heat; gradually stir in milk. Bring to a boil, stirring, and cook 2 minutes until thickened. Add cheese, half and half and grapes; cook, stirring, 5 minutes. Pour sauce over chicken and garnish with parsley.

Makes 4 servings.

CHICKEN STROGANOFF

1 pound skinned and boned chicken breast halves
1/4 cup butter or margarine
1 tablespoon olive oil
2 onions, thinly sliced
2 cups sliced button mushrooms
2 teaspoons Dijon-style mustard
1/3 cup sliced pickled gherkins
3/4 cup dairy sour cream
Salt and pepper
Noodles or rice, to serve
Chopped fresh parsley and paprika, to garnish

Place chicken breasts between 2 sheets of plastic wrap. Using a rolling pin, beat to flatten. Slice into 1-1/2″ × 1/2″ strips.

In a large skillet, heat half of the butter and oil. Add onions; cook until softened. Add mushrooms and cook 5 minutes. Remove from pan and set aside.

In the skillet, heat remaining butter and oil over high heat. Add chicken; cook, turning frequently, 6 to 8 minutes or until cooked through. Return onions and mushrooms to skillet. Stir in mustard, gherkins, cream, salt and pepper. Heat until hot, 3 to 4 minutes. Serve on a bed of noodles or rice and garnish with chopped fresh parsley and paprika.

Makes 4 servings.

—CHICKEN WITH MOUSSELINE—

MOUSSE:
3 ounces watercress leaves
3 ounces boned and skinned chicken breast half
Salt and pepper
2/3 cup whipping cream
8 chicken thighs, skinned and boned
SAUCE:
1 tablespoon vegetable oil
1 shallot, finely chopped
2/3 cup dry white wine
2/3 cup chicken stock
1/4 cup whipping cream
1 teaspoon chopped fresh tarragon or basil
1 teaspoon fresh lemon juice

Prepare Mousse: In a pan, blanch watercress in boiling salted water 15 seconds. Drain and refresh under cold water. Drain again and squeeze as dry as possible.

Into a food processor, put watercress. Add chicken breast and season with salt and pepper. Process mixture until pureed. Gradually pour in cream while the motor is running, taking care not to overbeat or cream will separate.

Preheat oven to 375F (190C). On a cutting board, lay chicken thighs. Season insides with salt and pepper. Add spoonfuls of Mousse. Roll flesh around Mousse to enclose it. Wrap each thigh in a square of oiled foil, sealing each one well. Place on a baking sheet. Bake 20 to 35 minutes or until the chicken is cooked through and Mousse is firm.

Meanwhile, prepare Sauce: In a saucepan, heat oil over low heat. Add shallot; cook until softened. Increase heat. Add wine and boil rapidly until quantity is reduced by half. Add chicken stock and continue reducing liquid to about 2/3 cup.

Add cream. Simmer, stirring constantly, 3 to 4 minutes or until sauce starts to thicken. Add tarragon and lemon juice and season with salt and pepper. Remove chicken thighs from the foil, arrange on a serving and top with sauce.

Makes 4 servings.

— SMOKED CHICKEN KEDGEREE —

2 tablespoons butter or margarine
1 teaspoon coriander seeds, crushed
1 onion, sliced
1 teaspoon ground coriander
2 teaspoons ground cumin
1/2 cup long-grain rice
1/2 cup red lentils
2-1/2 cups chicken stock
3 cups coarsely chopped smoked chicken
Juice of 1/2 lemon
1/2 cup plain yogurt
2 tablespoons chopped fresh parsley
2 hard-cooked eggs, coarsely chopped
1 lemon, sliced, to garnish
Mango chutney and poppadoms, to serve

In a large pan, melt butter. Add coriander seeds and onion. Cook over low heat until slightly softened. Stir in ground coriander, cumin, rice and lentils and coat well with butter. Pour in stock. Bring to a boil, then cover and simmer 10 minutes.

Remove lid. Add chicken and cook 10 minutes longer until all liquid is absorbed and rice and lentils are tender. Stir in lemon juice, yogurt, parsley and eggs. Heat until hot. Spoon into a warmed serving dish and garnish with lemon. Serve with mango chutney and poppadoms.

Makes 4 servings.

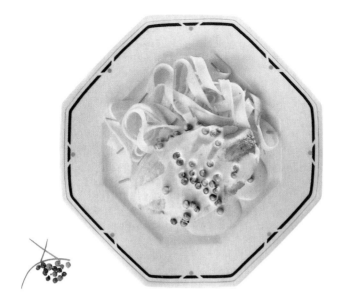

POULET AU POIVRE

2 tablespoons butter or margarine
1 tablespoon olive oil
4 skinned and boned chicken breast halves
3 tablespoons brandy
1 cup whipping cream
1 tablespoon green peppercorns in brine, drained
1 tablespoon pink peppercorns in brine, drained
Pinch of sugar
Salt

In a large skillet, heat butter and oil over medium-high heat. Add chicken; cook, turning, until browned on all sides.

Reduce heat, cover and cook 25 minutes longer, turning chicken occasionally. Remove chicken from skillet and set aside in a hot serving dish. Into skillet, pour brandy. Ignite brandy.

When the flames have died down, stir in cream, peppercorns, sugar and salt. Bring to a boil. Reduce heat, then simmer 2 to 3 minutes. Pour sauce over chicken and serve at once.

Makes 4 servings.

- CHICKEN WITH CHEESE SAUCE -

2 tablespoons vegetable oil
1 small onion, finely chopped
12 ounces chicken breast halves, sliced
6 ounces brown mushrooms
1-1/2 tablespoons all-purpose flour
2/3 cup dry white wine
2/3 cup chicken stock or water
5 ounces Boursin cheese
2 tablespoons chopped fresh parsley
Salt and pepper
1 pound fresh spinach noodles

In a large skillet, heat oil. Add onion and cook until transparent, stirring frequently. Add chicken and cook about 2 minutes. Add mushrooms. Cook 2 minutes or until chicken is cooked. Sprinkle flour over chicken and stir until all fat is absorbed. Remove from heat and slowly stir in white wine and stock or water. Return skillet to heat. Bring to a boil, stirring, until sauce thickens, then reduce heat.

Cut cheese into cubes. Add to sauce, stirring until melted. Add chopped parsley and season with salt and pepper. Cook pasta according to package directions until tender yet firm to the bite. Drain pasta well. Serve with chicken.

Makes 4 servings.

PAELLA

2 tablespoons butter or margarine
1 tablespoon vegetable oil
4 chicken drumsticks or thighs
1 large onion, sliced
2 garlic cloves, crushed
1 red bell pepper, sliced
1 green bell pepper, sliced
1-1/4 cups long-grain rice
2 teaspoons paprika
2-1/2 cups chicken stock
Pinch of saffron strands
6 ounces shelled cooked shrimp
6 ounces mussels, cleaned
1/2 cup frozen green peas
Salt and black pepper
Chopped fresh parsley and lime wedges, to garnish

In a paella pan, heat butter and oil. Add chicken; cook until golden, turning once. Remove from pan and set aside. Add onion, garlic and bell peppers and cook until slightly softened. Stir in rice and paprika. In another pan, bring stock to a boil. Add saffron and pour over rice mixture. Return chicken to pan and simmer 15 to 20 minutes.

Add shrimp, mussels and peas. Simmer 10 minutes longer or until all the liquid has been absorbed. Discard any mussels which remain closed. Season with salt and black pepper and garnish with chopped parsley and lime wedges.

Makes 4 servings.

—MUSHROOM RISOTTO—

1/4 cup butter or margarine
1 onion, finely chopped
1/2 pound skinned and boned chicken, sliced into strips
2 ounces prosciutto, cut into strips
3 cups mixed mushrooms, sliced
3 fresh rosemary sprigs
2 cups risotto rice
2/3 cup dry white wine
3-3/4 cups chicken stock
1-1/4 cups shredded mozzarella cheese
1/2 cup grated Parmesan cheese
Pepper

In a large pan, melt butter over low heat. Add onion; cook until softened. Increase heat; add chicken and brown on all sides. Stir in prosciutto, mushrooms, rosemary and rice and cook until rice is transparent.

Add wine. Cook over medium-low heat, stirring constantly, until wine is absorbed. Add stock half at a time; cook, stirring, until stock is absorbed and rice is creamy. Stir in mozzarella cheese and cook 5 minutes. Serve at once, sprinkled with Parmesan cheese and pepper.

Makes 4 servings.

STUFFED BRIOCHE

2 tablespoons butter or margarine
1 garlic clove, crushed
6 green onions, coarsely chopped
1 teaspoon green peppercorns in brine, drained
1 cup sliced button mushrooms
4 teaspoons dry vermouth
2/3 cup dairy sour cream
4 ounces cooked chicken, sliced
1 small red bell pepper, roasted, peeled and sliced
Salt and red (cayenne) pepper
1 tablespoon chopped fresh chervil
6 individual brioches, tops removed and centers
    scooped out

Preheat oven to 350F (175C). In a skillet,
melt butter. Add garlic, onions, peppercorns
and mushrooms; cook until onions soften.
Stir in vermouth. Stir in sour cream and
simmer until reduced and thickened. Stir in
chicken and pepper and cook 15 minutes.
Season with salt and cayenne. Stir in chervil.

Spoon chicken filling into brioches, replace
tops, place on a baking sheet and cover with
foil. Bake 10 minutes. Serve warm, garnished
with chervil sprigs.

Makes 6 servings.

──ITALIAN-STYLE CHICKEN ──

4 boned and skinned chicken breasts
8 prosciutto slices
6 ounces blue cheese, cut into 4 slices
Bunch of fresh sage
2 tablespoons olive oil
Freshly ground pepper
Sage sprigs, to garnish

With a sharp knife, cut each chicken breast in half. Flatten slightly by beating between 2 sheets of waxed paper with a rolling pin.

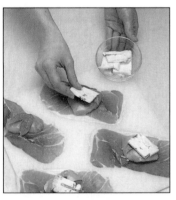

Lay prosciutto on a board. Put a piece of chicken in the middle of each slice. Place 2 or 3 fresh sage leaves on chicken and top with a slice of cheese. Wrap prosciutto around chicken to form a package.

In a skillet, heat oil. Add chicken. Fry 3 to 4 minutes on each side until chicken is cooked through and cheese melts. Garnish with sage sprigs.

Makes 4 servings.

CHICKEN PROVENÇAL

2 tablespoons butter or margarine
1 tablespoon vegetable oil
6 garlic cloves, unpeeled
4 chicken legs, cut in half
1/2 cup medium-dry sherry
1 (7-oz.) can chopped tomatoes
2 tablespoons tomato paste
2 tablespoons chopped fresh herbs
Salt and pepper
Oregano sprigs, to garnish

In a large skillet, heat butter and oil. Add garlic and chicken. Cook 15 minutes on one side until the chicken is half cooked through.

Add sherry and boil rapidly until reduced by half. Turn chicken pieces over. Continue to cook on high heat until sherry is reduced to a syrup.

Add tomatoes and tomato paste. Continue cooking 15 minutes longer until chicken is tender and sauce has reduced to a glaze. Add chopped herbs and season with a little salt and pepper. Serve with saffron rice and green beans. Garnish with oregano sprigs.

Makes 4 servings.

CHICKEN FRICASSEE

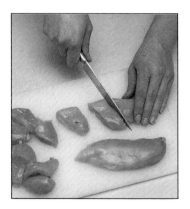

4 boned and skinned chicken breast halves
1/2 tablespoon vegetable oil
1 tablespoon butter or margarine
12 small shallots, halved
8 ounces shiitake mushrooms, sliced
1 tablespoon all-purpose flour
1/4 cup of dry white wine
2/3 cup chicken stock
2/3 cup whipping cream
1 tablespoon chopped fresh chervil or parsley
Juice of 1/2 lemon
Salt and pepper
Chervil leaves, to garnish

Cut each chicken breast half into 4 pieces. In a skillet, heat oil and butter. Add chicken and cook over high heat until golden. Remove from skillet and set aside. Add shallots to skillet. Cook 3 to 4 minutes until starting to turn golden. Add mushrooms and cook 2 minutes. Sprinkle flour over mushrooms and cook 1 minute. Gradually stir in white wine and chicken stock. Bring to a boil, stirring, and cook 2 minutes until sauce thickens slightly.

Return chicken and any juices to skillet. Add cream and simmer 10 to 12 minutes until chicken is tender. Add chervil, lemon juice, salt and pepper. Serve hot. Garnish with chervil.

Makes 4 servings.

- SPINACH & RICOTTA CHICKEN -

2 tablespoons olive oil
1 shallot, chopped
1 teaspoon fennel seeds
1/4 cup ricotta cheese
2 tablespoons pine nuts, toasted and chopped
2/3 cup finely chopped, cooked spinach, drained
4 chicken breast halves
Salt and pepper
8 bacon slices
1 garlic clove, crushed
1 (14-oz.) can chopped tomatoes
2 teaspoons tomato paste
2 teaspoons sugar
Salt and pepper
2 tablespoons chopped fresh basil

Preheat oven to 400F (205C). In a small pan, heat 1 tablespoon of the oil. Add shallot; cook until transparent. Add fennel seeds and cook 30 seconds. In a small bowl, mix shallot and fennel seeds with ricotta cheese and pine nuts. Add spinach to mixture; reserve. Lay chicken breast halves on a board. Slice each one through center, leaving edge uncut so each breast half can be opened flat. Season with salt and pepper. Spread 2 tablespoons of spinach mixture over half of each breast. Fold remaining side over filling.

Wrap 2 bacon slices around each chicken piece. Secure with wooden picks. Place in a small greased baking dish. Bake 15 to 20 minutes. Broil 2 to 3 minutes to crisp bacon. While chicken is cooking, add remaining oil to a small pan. Add garlic; cook 30 seconds. Add tomatoes, tomato paste, sugar, salt and pepper. Simmer 15 minutes or until thickened slightly. Add basil. Spoon over chicken and serve.

Makes 4 servings.

TARRAGON CHICKEN

2 tablespoons butter or margarine
1 tablespoon vegetable oil
4 large chicken breast halves, skinned
2 large leeks
2 tablespoons tarragon vinegar
2/3 cup white wine
1 cup chicken stock
1 large carrot
2/3 cup crème fraîche or whipping cream
1 teaspoon cornstarch
1 teaspoon tarragon-flavoured Dijon-style mustard
2 teaspoons fresh tarragon, chopped
Salt and pepper
Tarragon sprigs, to garnish

In a skillet, heat butter and oil. Add chicken; cook until golden on both sides. Remove from pan and drain on paper towels. Coarsely chop 1 leek. Add leek; cook until slightly softened. Add vinegar and boil rapidly until quantity is reduced by half. Add wine and stock. Return chicken to pan, cover and simmer 25 minutes. Cut remaining leek and the carrot into matchstick strips. Cook 4 to 5 minutes in separate pans of boiling, salted water. Drain; rinse under cold water. Drain again.

Remove chicken from skillet. Arrange on a warm serving dish. Strain cooking liquid. Bring to a boil. In a bowl, whisk together crème fraîche, cornstarch, mustard and 2 tablespoons pan juices. Return mixture to pan. Add carrots, leek and tarragon. Cook over low heat until sauce thickens. Season with salt and pepper. Spoon sauce over chicken pieces and garnish with tarragon sprigs.

Makes 4 servings.

——CHICKEN WITH YOGURT——

2/3 cup dry white wine
2 teaspoons dry mustard
3 tablespoons chopped fresh tarragon
4 skinned and boned chicken breast halves, cut into
    strips
1 tablespoon vegetable oil
1 tablespoon cornstarch
1 tablespoon water
3 tablespoons brandy
2/3 cup plain yogurt
Salt and pepper

In a medium-size bowl, mix together white wine, mustard and tarragon. Add chicken, mix well, cover and refrigerate 3 to 4 hours.

Drain chicken and reserve marinade. In a skillet, heat oil. Add chicken; cook quickly without browning. In a small bowl, mix cornstarch and water and add to the pan with brandy and reserved marinade.

Cook over medium heat 12 to 15 minutes or until chicken is cooked through. Add yogurt, heat through and season with salt and pepper. Serve hot.

Makes 4 servings.

LIVERS MARSALA

1 pound chicken livers, membranes removed
1 tablespoon all-purpose flour, seasoned
2 tablespoons butter or margarine
2 teaspoons olive oil
1 red onion, thinly sliced
1-1/2 cups sliced button mushrooms
2 ounces prosciutto, cut into thin slices
2 teaspoons chopped fresh thyme
1/3 cup Marsala wine
1 cup chicken stock
1 to 2 teaspoons Worcestershire sauce
2 teaspoons tomato paste
Salt and black pepper
Tagliatelle, to serve
2/3 cup dairy sour cream
Red (cayenne) pepper

Toss chicken livers in seasoned flour. In a skillet, heat butter and oil. Add onion; cook until softened. Remove from pan and set aside. Increase heat and fry floured livers until well browned. Reduce heat, return onion to pan and add any remaining flour, the mushrooms, prosciutto and thyme and stir well.

Add Marsala wine and stock. Bring to a boil, stirring constantly. Stir in Worcestershire sauce and tomato paste; season with salt and black pepper. Cook tagliatelle according to package directions, drain and arrange on a warmed serving plate. Top with livers, then sour cream. Sprinkle with a little cayenne and garnish with thyme.

Makes 4 servings.

CHICKEN WITH CRAB

4 skinned and boned chicken breast halves
6 ounces crabmeat
2 green onions, finely chopped
1 teaspoon tomato paste
Salt and pepper
1 tablespoon butter or margarine
1 shallot, finely chopped
1/4 cup brandy
1 tablespoon all-purpose flour
2 tablespoons dry white wine
1/2 cup chicken stock
6 ounces shelled cooked shrimp
1/4 cup crème fraîche or whipping cream
1-2 tablespoons lemon juice
1 tablespoon chopped fresh dill

Preheat oven to 400F (205C). Lay chicken breasts between 2 sheets of waxed paper. Beat with a rolling pin until about 1/4 inch thick. Mix crab with onions, tomato paste, salt and pepper. Place 2 to 3 tablespoons crab mixture along length of each chicken breast half. Roll up to enclose filling. Cut squares of foil larger than each chicken piece. Brush foil with oil and roll tightly around each chicken piece, twisting the ends to seal. Place in a baking dish and bake 12 to 15 minutes or until cooked through.

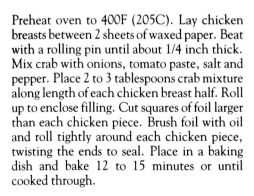

In a small pan, melt butter. Add shallot; cook 2 minutes. Add brandy and boil rapidly to reduce liquid by half. Stir in flour, then gradually add wine and stock. Bring to a boil; cook, stirring, until sauce has thickened. Add shrimp and crème fraîche and simmer 2 minutes. Add lemon juice and dill. Remove chicken from foil, adding any juices to sauce. Slice chicken breasts. Arrange on plates and top with sauce.

Makes 4 servings.

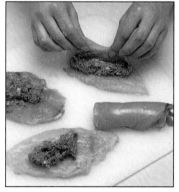

INDEX